A FLYING
START

Ron Pritchard

Published in 2021
by Ron Pritchard

© Copyright Ron Pritchard

ISBN: 978-1-913898-14-4

Book design by Russell Holden
www.pixeltweakspublications.com

 Pixel Tweaks Publications
SELF PUBLISHING MADE SIMPLE

INTRODUCTION

At the time of being born, there was no such thing as the wonderful NHS as we know it today, hence my flying start.

After that my life has been quite a roller coaster, I do hope you enjoy my life experiences with me, no one was hurt, only my pride mixed with a little bit of fear and trepidation.

May I say a big thank you to Mr Ken Moore for his proofreading and literary support! Dean and Jane and for their help with the front cover, Russell Holden for his inside graphics and guidance in putting this book together.

All the proceeds after initial expenses from this little book will be going to our local Hospice as they do such a great job for our little town of Ulverston and surrounding area.

The pages that follow cover some of the situations and anecdotes encountered.

All the stories are true; only the names have been changed to protect the author!

I'd like to thank my wife, Margaret, for letting me back in each time I came home and laughing at my stories.

Thanks also go to my daughter, Elaine, for deciphering my handwriting and adding yet another chapter.

CONTENTS

A FLYING START

I was born in the hospital in Harrogate simply because I wished to be close to Mum. Only I was quite premature. Mum delivered me with no difficulty. Apparently I was extremely small, the male midwife held me by the ankle and threw me on the bed stating 'that thing will not live long'. Mum was not accepting that, having had six children before me so she had had quite a bit of practice.

Mum took me home and popped me in a shoe box as I only weighed the same as a small bag of sugar. In time I progressed to being given a drawer to sleep in. So fortunately I began to thrive and here I am today.

The moral of this is ***do not take other people on face value.***

Going back to when mum used to take me to the shop where she worked; this was during the second world war. I used to hinder when I could, me thinking I was being of some use.

I remembered very little of the war, only when we had to move from Whitby to within eight miles south of Leeds

1

this was towards the end of the war. We heard the air raid sirens from time to time coming from Leeds; living in a mining village there were still quite a number of men about, mining being a reserved occupation. I do remember the clogs going past about five-thirty in the morning, a decent wake up call, well before you needed one. Everything went well until demob day, when father turned up on our doorstep along with a friend, up until by this time I had never met father? I was five years old, mum said, (which one do you think is your dad?); Not liking the look of what turned out to be father I chose the other chap, thinking I would end up living with the one I had chosen. No such luck, I'm sure Dad never forgave me.

There were seven children in the family. I say, children, by the time I was five, my eldest sister was seventeen. There were four sisters and three brothers. Two sisters were just before me in age, and you can imagine I wasn't too happy about getting hand me downs; my older brother could never understand why his sisters had three brothers, and he only had two.

A consequence of living in a small mining village throughout our lives, we had all attended the same primary school. Unfortunately, one teacher had taught five of my family before it was my turn. Whenever I had done something wrong or had difficulty with a subject I was confronted with, your so and so had no problem doing this. The crunch came when she said, "Even your Dennis could do this" (I taught him how to tie his shoelaces), and he was eight years older than me. I cried for a week.

When I escaped the confines of the house, I could be anywhere! For example, a nearby farm, the wind cover wood, the local reservoir going anywhere, unlike today; unfortunately, children are unable to be let loose on their own. Both my parents thought I was a little horror; I must admit I did have the ability to get into trouble quite quickly. So here we go. Still quite young, it was time for me to attended Sunday school; I had a sister on either side leading me to church. On entering this quite dark, imposing building, my sisters veered off to the right and sent me to catch up with an elderly lady who they said would take me for my Sunday school lesson; I had no sooner caught up with her when she grabbed my hand and headed off down a set of dark steps, well I had been told hell was down below, and if I was naughty that was where I would finish up, my little mind was thinking I'm much too young for this place, the lady holding my hand must have wondered what on earth had happened as I took flight and disappeared. All the way home I was promising "I'll be good, I'll be good, I'll be good in future". It's a little bit like a new years resolution– it doesn't last long.

UP & AWAY

Even at a young age, I was fascinated by wheels, possibly because we ran a taxi service; for example, I would make things such as a bogey (or a four-wheeled trolly). I also had roller skates and a bicycle. Let me start with the bogey; we must remember there were far fewer vehicles on the roads in those days we often used the minor roads to play on. On this particular occasion, I was travelling quite quickly down one of the narrow country roads.

Laying down, using my hands on the crossbar to steer, I noticed a milk collection wagon parked in my path when I looked up. Having no room to manoeuvre around said vehicle, I went underneath, hoping to miss the back axle, no problem! Can you imagine the look on the drivers face when this thing shot out from under his vehicle, I do remember hearing a few expletives, though.

My next episode involved the same bogey, it was a very warm summers day, and I was stripped down for racing in a T-shirt and shorts. There was a steep grassy bank close to our house, with a path running through it and very large nettles on either side. I was travelling reasonably well until one of my front wheels caught the edge of the path! Isn't it amazing how quickly you can still travel when you leave your mode of transport? In this case, it was through the nettles for what must have been thirty yards. The bogey was well and truly forgotten as I very gingerly made my way home.

Mum was not very impressed on seeing this not so little Michelin man entering the house.

Unfortunately, Mum was never keen on taking us to the doctors or the hospital, so it was left to one of my brothers or sisters to call on Mrs Riley, our neighbour; off we went on the bus, as you can imagine, I was unable to sit down, also feeling quite poorly. I knew nothing about anaphylactic shock in those days.

There was a lot of scurrying about on my entering the hospital; and something was mentioned about why my mother hadn't rung for an ambulance.

I was still unable to sit or lay down, and everything became a bit vague after that. I am sure that they did not use an injection; otherwise, they would have had to hold me down with a piece of string. On this occasion, my visit to the hospital lasted a number of days.

We now move on to the bicycle. This was what I called an AJS (all junk stuck together), which was anything you could lay your hands on in those days. This particular one was classed as a 'sit up and beg' with the handlebars and a seat that was a bit on the high side with the seat being higher than my little legs; consequently, I used to slide from one side of the saddle to the other.

One day I was asked to run an errand to the local shop, this was up a hill at the top of the village. While riding back down the hill, a young person ran out from behind a hedge right into my bike frame, the bike stopped, but I kept going straight over the handlebars, face-first onto a newly gravelled road. I knew I had done some damage, how much I was about to find out. Again the bike was forgotten, as I made my way home very slowly. Mum was coming out of the house just as I was approaching; she took one look at me and promptly fainted. I don't think she was expecting her son to be able to smile vertically as well as horizontally. So it was back to Mrs Riley to ask her to take me to the doctors. By this time, I had a tea towel covering my face. Mrs Riley said she had better have a look! "Goodness gracious, yes, we had better get you to the doctor and quick".

Going along on the bus this time, at least I could sit down. People were curious as to what had happened, so I showed them; they did not stare for long; they turned away very quickly, looking somewhat shaken. The nurse in the doctor's surgery assessed my injury and took me through to see the doctor right away. My usual doctor was away, so a locum was standing in for her, the only thing was he was eighty if he was a day and he had very shaky hands, I was seated on a chair with my back to the wall as he headed toward me with his needle and thread; his hands were shaking so much I had difficulty trying to keep my head in time with him. At one stage, I was standing on the chair with him trying to follow me. And by this time, Mrs Riley had left the room looking quite ill. He eventually struggled to get three stitches in place, then said, "Are thinking about becoming a film star? If so I will put another two stitches in". I believe the second word I replied with was "off".

I arrived home as tea was being served, my brothers trying hard to make me laugh, which is quite tricky with your upper lip sewn up. This was not quite the end of the affair. After about ten days, I needed to go back to have the stitches removed.

My regular doctor asked:

"Who on earth put these in?"
I said, "The locum, why?"
"I am really going to struggle to remove them".

And she did. After about five minutes, I found myself coming round laying on the floor. Fortunately, she had managed to remove the last of them while I was spark out. The strange thing is when I was having them put in, I had stayed awake, which must have been a far more dramatic experience.

SCHOOL DAYS

Our local primary school was affectionately called Swillington Tin Can Tech because it was constructed of 'wriggly tin', or if you prefer, corrugated iron sheets. It was brrrrr cold in winter, with all the pupils vying for the nearest position to the pot-bellied stove—no central heating in those days.

Boys wore short trousers until they were about fourteen years old. It must have been something to do with the cost of clothes. Not the best of things to wear on a cold winters day, especially doing sports with a bat or when a ball hits you on the leg, leaving an impression of the object. When asked what you enjoyed most about school ("playtimes") on one occasion during playtime, I was sitting on a wall with my legs not quite reaching the floor; there were spikes on the wall, and I was sitting between them. When the class bell went I jumped off the wall, not quite clearing the spikes. I hung there for a little while before a tearing sound came, dumping me on my hands and knees. I gave a very good Impression of a young

Indian brave with my shorts swinging freely front and back. I was unsure whether to go into the classroom and face the humiliation, holding the material together, or going straight home, whichever way I would come face to face with Mother's wrath. I postponed the inevitable and crept into the classroom. Not the best idea!

I am sure one of our male teachers was a masochist; he had this thin, willowy cane he would hold while walking too and fro, swishing it from left to right. This certainly gave him the upper hand. We boys would try different remedies to ward off the pain of the cane; (I needed a remedy more than most). It would depend as to whether the cane was going to be directed toward your hand or your backside. Remedies included:

Licking your hand before contact

Putting a piece of horsehair on your hand

A smear of vaseline to direct the cane off your limb

Anything between your trousers and your skin

(although this had to be very inconspicuous, or it was taken away, followed by an extra whack).

Believe you me, nothing worked.

The local ice cream van parked just outside the school gates. It was there, for the ones who could afford to buy one. I became very familiar with the vendor, and on one occasion, I cajoled him into letting me have some dry ice. This product is strange because dry ice burns. The piece he gave me I had to be shuffled from one hand to the other to keep me from letting go of it. It was lunchtime, so there was no one in the classroom, I diligently broke this ice into very small pieces and popped a piece in each ink well on all the desks, then calmly went back outside. Returning into the class after the lunch break, the teacher's face and actions were a picture to behold. He was jumping up and down with a very red face.

"Who?" He was saying, while every inkwell had a spiral of smoke coming up from it. I am sure my appearance must have given me away because I must have been the only one looking quite pleased with themselves. He homed in on me right away, oh no!! Not the dreaded cane, today he had no cane handy, so he ordered me to go outside to break a thin branch off a bush. Hmm, now which one do you choose? I chose one with plenty of leaves. He whipped out his knife and stripped every leaf and stem before he proceeded to use it. However, the accolades I received from my compatriots pretty well made up for my discomfort.

I was never one for staying in bed in a morning (being frightened of missing something, I suppose), especially at weekends. One Sunday morning, I was up and dressed

in my Sunday best, mooching about waiting for everyone else to emerge. No, I cannot wait any longer!! So I found my fishing net and a jam jar, and off I went down to the reservoir to catch some Sticklebacks and Reddies.

It was a lovely summer morning as I sat there with my net catching nothing, so I thought I would shin along the outlet pipe to be nearer the action. There I was, just stretching out beyond my reach when the most unexpected happened; I gently slid around the pipe and splash. Things seemed to happen in slow motion; however, the end result was the same I was wet through from feet to breakfast time.

I am sure you can visualise this young feller sitting on the grass bank completely naked, with all his clothing hanging on the surrounding bushes, looking like semaphore. I also had to keep an ear on the church clock, this was the only way I had of keeping in touch with the time, bearing in mind I was due to go to Sunday school. I made it with minutes to spare and a few sideways glances from the family. I was sure I had got away with it until Mum looked down at my shoes.

"And how did they get into that state?"
"I went through some water."
"Water? it hasn't rained for two months!"

I remember being grounded for quite a while, not until after I had tasted the slipper.

In my later school years, Father decided he would get some goose eggs. These we placed under a broody hen, there were six of them, five hatched out. I looked after them from the start, and I did not know that there was such a thing as bonding; however, this is what must have happened because I had become their friend, each one named, of course. We lived on a corner of a main road, so whenever I came home from school, there was hell's own chorus as I turned this corner. They kept this up until I went up to them, petted and talked to them.

If dad was after me for any misdemeanour, I would go into the pen with the geese, and he would not dare to come in for fear of getting attacked. He would stand outside shouting," you cannot stay in there forever; I will have you when you come out!'" I just hoped he had calmed down by the time I came out; he didn't.

As and when I went to the local shops, I would take them with me. They would walk along behind me in a line. When I arrived at the shop, they would just stand outside until I came out, off we would go again. I never had any problems with the village bullies while I had the geese with me. If I had any problems with said bullies, I would threaten them with a visit from my geese, and it never came to that. Just before one Christmas, father had the local butcher come around and take three of the geese, without my knowledge, so there were only two left. I bawled my eyes out; also, Christmas was a non-event for me. The two that were left must have felt it as much as me, it was ages before they started eating, and I spent a great deal of time with them, for their comfort and mine. It was never the same again. Fortunately, they appeared to realise I was not to blame for the loss of the others, so they stayed very close to me.

SWIMMING

Mum had a thing about any of us going in or near water, and as you know with children, the last thing you want to hear is "do not."

So at every opportunity, we were stripped down and ready for the off, either down to the canal or a nearby quarry

One time while messing about in the quarry, we happened on something floating a little bit away from the edge. One or two of the others lads were better swimmers than me, so they swam out to investigate.

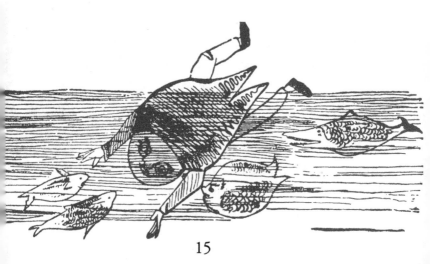

On reaching this object there was an unholy scream followed by those two tearing back to shore at Olympic speed, unable to say anything. On reaching the bank, it took us a while to make any sense from them, even then it came out like "there-there-there, is somebody floating out there, literally". Oh, eck what do we do now? We had what could only be a dead body out there and two gibbering wrecks on the bank. It took us quite a while to settle them down and figure what to do next—don't forget we were not supposed to be near water, so we went to tell a policeman rather than risk going home with the news.

The trouble is policemen do not keep their gob shut; the first thing they did was inform our parents, so it didn't do any good going to them; we still got the slipper and sent to bed.

Our other haunt was the nearby canal, this waterway transported coal in tubs pulled by a barge from the nearby mines to a power station on the outskirts of Leeds. The canal was handy enough, approx a mile from home at the bottom of a hill. We would sit on the canal side, remove our clothes and tie them in a bundle.

During our splashing about, someone had to keep an eye out for the lock keeper. Most of the time, we would get away with it. Only occasionally, by means of stealth, he would get too close for comfort. Instead of waiting until he reached us, he would let out such a roar, and we very quickly popped out of the water, grabbed our clothes and took off up the hill; there we would be up to six little bare bottoms wiggling up the hill tag-lag as fast as we could. He would carry on shouting and waving his stick about as we receded into the distance.

My elder brother used to take several friends to the swimming baths each Sunday, and I would pester him to take me. He said he would take me once I had learned to swim. I had managed to swim about three to four yards, I told him I had learned to swim, I just didn't tell him how far, and reluctantly he let me tag along. Feeling very grown-up until we reached the pool where he and a friend took me down to the deep end, they picked me up and threw me in. The moral of that story is, wait until you are ready before you mouth off. I was close to drowning before they elected to drag me out, coughing and spluttering.

When we were at the seaside we would go down to the beach, if it was hot we would spend time in the water, understandable mother was very reluctant to let us go in the water at all, so I would say to Father, "How far out can I go?" He would say, "Keep going until your hat floats!" The thing is, I'm not so sure if he meant it. We used to joke if Father had been the one teaching us to swim the hardest part would be getting out of the sack first, and thankfully for us, he was unable to swim.

When I was able to swim reasonably well, a group of us lads used to bike to an outside swimming pool, or as they were called in those days, 'lidos'. It was about fifteen miles away, so we were ready for a cool down by the time we arrived. Some of us would be suitably attired, but others not so. Peter Hut had to borrow a pair of his dad's trunks; Peter had a twenty-inch waist while his dad's waist would be nearer forty. In order to overcome this disparity, Peter held them up with an elastic snake belt. Now Peter was one of our stars; he climbed up onto the diving board and effected one of the cleanest dives you could ever witness, the only thing was his belt stayed put, but his trunks did not; they bobbed up and down on the surface. I was sitting on the poolside when this happened. In a flash, I was in the pool and back out nearly before Peter surfaced. He was blissfully unaware that anything was wrong. By now, I was sitting on the opposite side, waving his trunks in the air. His comments went something like, "would you please throw them back". What do you think? It was sport for quite a while.

When I was a teenager, as well as having a taxi business, we also had a number of caravans sited at Primrose Valley near Filey in North Yorkshire; this was sixty-four miles from where we lived. On a weekend our taxis would transport holidaymakers to and from their home to the resort. The family already staying in the vans would have to vacate by ten-thirty in order to allow the cleaning staff time to clean and refresh the van. In some instances, you would think they had occupied it for six months,

However, we will not go into that side of things. My brother and I used to go over on a Friday evening to prepare them for the next holidaymakers. We would go over on our pushbikes the night before and stay in a tent. If we were early enough, we ran along the beach to filey to see a film then run back. The cramp was excruciating; in fact, on one occasion, I got cramp in my leg while in the cinema, my leg shot under the chair in front. Would you believe they decided to stand up at the same time and lift their seat into the upright position? This meant I found myself standing up very quickly indeed, talk about discomfort; wow!

My friend and I arranged to go on a camping holiday, using our bicycles. We set off from home; this was from eight miles south of Leeds. We cycled up to Windermere, with the camping gear stashed on the bikes, if they fell over, it took both of us to lift it upright. We managed to do the distance in a day; needless to say, we were a little creamed crackered when we arrived at our destination.

Food well! By the time we had erected the tent, we had no strength left to bother making anything to eat. Mind you, the food we did make left a lot to be desired. We were camping on what might be best described as on a shoestring – mind you, some of our food tasted like them. Our cooked meals were all made in one pan on a primus stove; I will let you use your imagination.

Four days camped on the shores of Windermere; we were on the road again, heading for Southport. This was a much better ride with not so many hills. We pitched our tent on the sand dunes but only for one night. I had never heard of sand fleas (we did then), and our warm little bodies must have been too much of a temptation for them. We thought we had chickenpox and itching like fury.

We galloped, well cycled, around the town looking for a chemist; we then covered ourselves with chamomile lotion until we looked like a couple of ghosts, trying very hard to keep a very low profile. Needless to say, one night on the sand dunes was plenty enough. Even the grassy areas were packed with wildlife. It was time to pack up and move on.

We headed out of sunny Southport towards the Penninies. The trip was quite a challenge as it is all uphill down there. We pushed our bikes for three miles plus, night was drawing in, and we were getting hungry. Our trusty Primus stove was put to use, about all we had was placed in a pan, warmed up and eaten, it did not matter what it was it all went down the same way.

By the time we had finished eating, we were far too tired to pitch the tent, so we threw the tent on the ground, crawled into our sleeping bags, wrapped ourselves up and fell asleep. On lifting my head the following morning, we had company, at about a distance of ten yards and standing facing us stood a row of sheep. I awoke brian saying we were surrounded by Indians; it was one of his quickest wake-up calls. They must have given us a visit during the night; just about everything was trodden on; even our bedding had little hoof marks in between our limbs. Now it is time to go home. When we arrived home, we had the mould for a saddle, so we stayed off the bikes for quite a while until the funny walk improved.

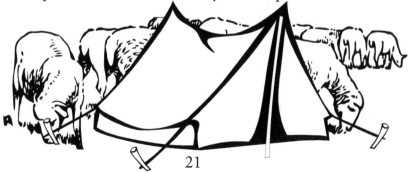

SPORTS AT SCHOOL

We were encouraged to take up a variety of sports until you found one that might suit you.

I first tried cricket, I was sent out to be a fielder, which is when I discovered just how hard the ball was. Our games master had this view that if you throw the ball straight at someone's face, there is a good chance they would catch it. The alternative was to duck very quickly, or else on my first game, the ball left the bat and went quite high, heading toward me. I was stood rooted to the spot with my hands together; this missile missed my hands completely, and it hit my kneecap—no more cricket for me.

Next up was rounders; at least the ball was not quite as hard. I started off well until the time came for me to bat. There I was waiting my turn in line until the girl in front of me stepped up to bat, the bowler bowled, the girl did at least a 360-degree arc, missed the ball completely promptly let go of the bat, which just about embedded into my forehead—no more rounders for me.

If we were caught fighting in the playground, the games teacher would take us both into the gym, and he would then hand out boxing gloves. The rest of the school were not allowed in the room; however, every window was full of faces.

Whoever won on the day was seconded onto the boxing team, so here I was, part of this sport. I took to the sport well. I suppose having two quite older brothers and a vindictive father, who, when having a bad day, would take their frustration out of me, this enabled me to take whatever boy's my age were likely to dish out,

I only lost three fights during my time boxing, one occasion, my opposite number was one of the thinnest boys I ever come across, so I was not too worried, I should have been, the bell went, before I had time to stand up he was in front of me, his hands were like pistons, I did not know how to respond. This happened for three rounds, in which time I hit him twice, so I well and truly lost on points.

The second time we appeared to be well-matched in size, the ring craft this boy showed was well out of my class. While talking to him later, it turns out he was a nephew of bruce woodcock, a professional boxer who had taught him a lot of the ways of boxing.

On another occasion, we were sat waiting for the bell to go, the boy opposite me looked a bit nervous, the bell went he stood up and instantly threw his arms out in front of him, his gloves shot off, he then high tailed it up the passage and away.

I wondered how he came to be sat facing me in the first place. We were supposed to be fairly evenly matched beforehand.

At playtime, we used to enjoy making a slide when it was icy. This stretched diagonally across what would be the tarmac part of our playground. As time went on, this became longer and longer until it reached the school wall. If you managed to make it to the end, you stopped by hitting this wall, and as I mentioned, it was wiggly tin, so you would rattle down these ridges before you stopped. *"Ow, ow, ow, ow"* was the stopping cry.

It was only after someone was taken to hospital that the slide was sanded.

On one occasion, while I was traversing said slide, one of the girls decided she would walk across "oops" we went down together without losing speed, being a thoughtful soul, I turned around before we reached the wall, I hit the wall and she hit me, guess who came off worst, a bonus, no bones broken.

After school, during this cold weather, we would take our sledges to a hill that was called the Betty log (don't ask). This hill had one or two trees scattered about, also a stream at the bottom. Most of the time, we avoided the trees. The stream was something else, your choices were to stop or hit the water. This meant a walk home freezing cold and in disgrace.

We in our majesty would build a bridge over this stream using very large snowballs, these being made by rolling the snow down the hill. Three would do the job. We had options now; we either stopped, turned or went over the bridge. We never realised the stream was making its way through our bridge. The realisation came with someone not making it across, the bridge caved in, and they had a ducking. So off home they went.

We would try our version of off-road scrambling. A little 50cc motorbike seemed a very likely machine the problem was the gearbox was caput, so we bypassed the box and connected the drive chain straight to the engine, so we placed the bike on its stand then joe climbed aboard with the engine revving we (the 'royal' we) standing behind gave the bike a very gentle push everything happened, this bike decided to bury itself into the ground resulting in brian and I completely covered in sh/one/t before it decided to take off, through the muck and the grime I saw joe hanging on for dear life in a horizontal position, I am sure had he not run out of petrol he would have finished up in the next county.

So back to the drawing board, we decided four wheels would be safer than two. After a bit of searching through scrap yards, we came across a little Standard Ten. Unfortunately, the engine was caput, so we were on the prowl for another engine we may be able to fit into the space. We found one, although it was slightly larger than the one we removed. After quite a bit of huffing and puffing, we eventually managed to replace the new engine and gearbox well new to us. What about a test drive; I said, what about a test drive. As you can imagine, the engine did not start the first time. After delving back into the working Brum-Brum, yes, we have lift off. Round and round the farmer's dirt track, luckily, one of our team was this farmers son. Although we had to use the brakes, we did not realise they were operated with cables, and after a few time, the cables stretched, making it impossible to stop the car. So it was a case of cruising to a stop

Coming to the end of school days, my last school report was a bit, how would you say, negative – along the lines of 'to say this person is about to enter the workaday world god help him!' Needless to say, this did not reach the eyes of my parents, even with such a negative start.

STARTING WORK

I enrolled as an apprentice at a garage in the next village approx two miles away, so I was able to use my bike. They say children can be unkind; I soon realised nowhere near the way adults can be. At school, for instance, my nickname was 'Pilch', the first week at work, it became 'Sir Slantalot' because I have scoliosis, which gives cause to a bend in my spine. This is something I had no control over, so hearing this was very hurtful.

I quickly came across words I never knew existed. I started by asking my older brothers what the terms meant, not the best idea.

With me being the new boy, the person that started, say six months before me, not only gave a big sigh of relief because the pressure was off him, but he could now torment me along with all the others.

Just before tea breaks, the new boy had to collect orders from everyone then go to the cafe next door, whoa betide any mix-ups or spillages, or worse still breakages. Some had the habit of throwing a cup from the other end of the workshop then would shout "Incoming" when it was in the air. You would have to look up to see which direction the cup was heading (hopefully yours), they would see if they could manage to get it through the roof supports if they hit the supports they had to pay for it, but if you missed catching it, you had to pay. I quickly realised nothing was fair.

Some of the mechanics had their own enamel mugs; however, one was more of a torment than the others. One day I was feeling a bit teed off with him, so I drilled a small hole in the bottom of his mug (this was easier said than done), and so each time he took a drink, it would dribble down his overalls. My laughing soon subsided when I had to buy him another mug, dash.

I am fairly bright, but the only thing is I never knew when to give up. On another occasion, I not only drilled a hole in the mug I screwed it to the bench; as you can imagine, it caused an uproar when he tried to pick it up to have a drink, partly because the other guy's did not know what I had done, it took a while for him to realise it was well and truly fastened down. Another mug to buy. Ahh well.

Sweets and chocolate were in short supply in those days, I had saved up and bought myself a Mars bar. I popped it into the top pocket of my overalls and carried on working. As time passed, some items I had dismantled needed cleaning. There was a large square tank holding a mixture of paraffin and petrol we used for this work, I leaned over to start the cleaning process, then yes, you have guessed it, the bar dropped into the mixture, quickly retrieved by me, wrapper off in a flash, too late it tasted of paraffin, yuk.

It was difficult to keep the place warm in winter; every time a car came in or out, the garage became very cold. On a lunchtime in winter, we would all huddle in the boiler house next to a coke stove. We usually took sandwiches but Friday was fish and chip day. As you can imagine in those days, we looked as black as crows, some more so than others. After lunch on a Friday, we always came out of the boiler house with two very clean fingers. On one occasion, Willy dropped his fish in the coke and ash residue; he picked it up, wiped it on his overalls and carried on eating it. The batter sounded much crisper than it had before. Hey, waste not want not, money was tight on an apprentice wage.

Ken came in one Friday bragging about having a home-made meat and potato pie. He had placed it on top of the stove first thing so that it would be warm in time for lunch. He was a pain all morning going on about this pie.

The top of this stove was slightly domed, and as the pie heated up, it must have

leaked a little bit because five minutes before lunchtime, it slid off onto the floor upside down so he shouted "Just a minute bring me some fish and chips"... shame!

As mentioned earlier, they were not a caring bunch. On one occasion, George was working on a car heater, and these happened to be quite scarce in the fifties. On lifting the bonnet, there was an open box with the heater fan inside; George had his hand inside adjusting the cable, the fan was working at the time. George with screwdriver in hand when it slipped off the screw head, then bbbbrrrp his hand went inside. Putting said hand behind his back, he went up to Vernon and asked, "How many fingers have I on this hand?" Vernon, not knowing what had happened, said, "Three and a half!" Whereby George promptly fainted—smack OW! The only injury he sustained was where he hit the floor face first, so it was still a hospital job.

As time passed, I was no longer the new boy, another young lad called Joe started, and he must have had a rather different upbringing to me, as he was gobbie, right from the start.

Not a clever thing to be in front of your peers; they had seen it all before. One day Joe had really become very annoying, so when everyone, except the ones on the late shift, picked Joe up and transferred him to a bench at the far end of the garage, this was around a corner, we put him on the bench, then fastened his overall sleeve cuffs in the vice, followed by the bottom of his trouser legs into another vice approx 5ft 6in away, placed some masking tape over his mouth and bid him goodnight. The manager on his rounds an hour later spotted Joe in his predicament and elected to set him free. Next morning neither Joe nor the manager mentioned this incident, the manager knowing we would all own up to this.

Joe and I became quite friendly, and we used to travel to work and back on a tandem. When we got the hang of synchronising our balance and peddling, we could work up quite a turn of speed and creating a few near mishaps. A few cars never saw us coming alongside them; they did things that led to us having to make a few very sudden moves.

The riding together worked well; unfortunately, after I dropped Joe off about half a mile from home, there was quite a steep hill.

This became a drag, so the tandem was abandoned in favour of a motorbike. Joe acquired one of his own.

Having this new steed (well, new to me), I was invariably running late for work, so I had to get a move on. On one occasion, coming toward a bus stop, I spied Ken. I knew he would be late for work, so from 30 plus miles an hour, I spun round in the road stopping next to where he was stood. "Jump on, Ken", I shouted. His second word was "OFF!" I said, "You are going to be very late and have time docked off your day". He finally agreed to jump on, then off we went. I stopped at some traffic lights then set off again. I turned and shouted, "you OK Ken? Ken? oh no, Ken!"

So around in the road again and headed back to find him stood brushing himself down.

Apparently, when we were stationary at the lights he stood up to tuck his coat under himself and as I set off he sat down on the road.

He was even later for work than he would originally been. When he did turn up, not only did he blame me, but I was an absolute idiot and should not be allowed on the road.

On one occasion I went back with Joe to his house in the evening. Having stayed late I had to get home so I went out to kick the bike to see a flame about a yard long shoot out of the exhaust manifold; not only was it close to setting my trouser leg on fire the noise was horrendous. You maybe don't react as quite as you should do in these circumstances, by which time just about every upstairs window opened with a few choice words being sent forth. Someone had kindly knocked my bike over and knocked the exhaust off. It took a bit of sorting out in the dark; this was after I had pushed it well away from the houses.

On one occasion, my family had gone off for the weekend, so Joe came to stay. You can imagine what two teenagers were like. Having messed about most of the day we went off to bed but with no chance of sleeping we soon got up again and went outside into a big greenhouse where there was a dim light (this helped the Chrysanthemums to grow).

While we were in there a voice said,
"Hello what is going on here", not a local policeman,
oh yes it was, quick as a flash I said we were weeding,
"weeding... at 2am?"
I said
"well you cannot weed in bed, can
you?"
Right Pritchard, talk your way out of
that.

APPRENTICESHIP & COLLEGE

As part of our apprenticeship, we were expected to attend college one day a week, and one evening for up to five years. This was the first time in our lives we were called 'Mister' at least it made us feel important.

We must have been very slow learners in those days, either that or the employers wanted a few more years out of us at apprentice rates. However, we did get a good grounding!

Covering things like panel beating, spray painting and welding. The thing was if you did not pass onto the following year after the second attempt at college, you lost your place at work.

One guy had been in the first year for four years, and we think because his father owned a large garage and was on the governing panel, his son got dispensation. It was said they had to burn the college down to get him to move on.

I am sure you can imagine, a few pranks were played in college, certainly on our day release. We were allowed out to go for lunch. I nearly always went to the same cafe for their version of Welsh rarebit; at least it was clean and cheap. Whoever arrived back from lunch did not always revise– far from it; they caused the most mayhem.

Like fastening your desktop down or tying two chairs together so if one moved, so did your partner's.

We were located on the second floor on a very busy road, both vehicles and footfall. Somebody thought it was a good idea to hang someone's case out of the window, never taking into account it was raining. When the student finally located it and eased the case up, it decided to fly open, discharging its belongings onto the footpath below. He arrived back with this sodden and trodden-on mess, and he was very, very unhappy. The pranks eased off for quite a while after that although it was not the end of them.

The classroom had a rope block and tackle at the back, so I wound it out as far as it would go and then hooked it onto a chair near the front of the class, me sitting at the back started to pull gently on the rope a little at a time. This was really good to watch the person's chair started creeping backwards; he did not realise what was happening until he was pushing the desk of the guy behind him, and it dawned on them. At the end of class, no one had to be asked twice to leave. It was up and away, but on this occasion, not for this chap, he jumped up, and there was a ripping sound someone had quietly hooked a thin rope onto his pocket tied to a 50lb weight on the floor – enough said.

During my time at college, I used a selection of transport; to begin with, it was a pushbike. Living eight miles away, I would always try to beat the bus home. To make it fair, I would set off at the same time. On one occasion, I was stood between the bus and the kerb talking to a friend at the bus stop. Just as the bus started to pull away, I was steadying myself on the bus side, touching the bus as he pulled away I misjudged my timing as I put my hand out for the last time, only the bus moved away quicker than I thought, leaving me in a heap on the floor. On the lighter side, I always won the bus.

TRANSPORTATION

My next mode of transport was a motorbike.

Two episodes stand out in my mind; I was talking to a girl who lived down our street, so I offered her a lift home; as we headed out of Leeds, she said, "is this the best you can do? I may as well used the bus", no second telling, as we headed toward Sturtan humpback bridge I open the throttle and we hit the bridge at about 65 mile per hour. I was very surprised when the bike left the ground. I'm thinking *I do hope this thing lands straight and safely.* This happened as smooth as silk, would you believe Daphne never said another word all the way home. When we stopped she leapt off the bike and did a strange walk to her house. Can you believe she would never go on the bike again?

Another incident– I was heading toward the bike in the underground car park after night school. As I approached, the bike looked bigger than it should have at the back. It was! There was a guy sat behind removing my rear light unit "what the ..." he said "someone has nicked my light" so I thought I would have this one" ... I think not.

Heading to college one day, it was very foggy (in those days, it was not just foggy; they were peasoupers called smog). I came over a hill to see a bus parked. I reckon he was picking passengers up so it was too dangerous to pass; I just sat there twiddling my thumbs. The next thing I was up in the air as far as the upper floor of the bus, I did not have time to wave to the passengers, what goes up must come down and all that.

I landed on my back, half on the road and half on the pavement – not so good. It took quite a while for the ambulance to come then there was a lot of debate relating to my back as I was doing my best to tell them about my condition. They were saying things like, "You take it easy you have had a very nasty knock" I was then heading for the ambulance on a stretcher saying:

"What about my bike?"

Fortunately, after x-rays, they come to the conclusion that I had been very badly bruised; I just required a few days rest.

Apparently, what had happened was that a van came over the hill much quicker than he should and slammed into me. My double seat flicked up in the middle and ejected me from my seat. Had it not, I would have been squashed between the van and the bus. Human nature is funny when my neighbours were saying I knew he would come to grief on that thing. The bike was returned home for me to straighten it out.

Now was the time for me to learn to drive a car. My driving instructor was a lady. I am sure she had taught mechanics in the past, so there was to quarter given. For example, if I hovered my foot over the clutch for more than two seconds, the spine of her very thick diary came down on my thigh. Likewise, if my hand did not leave the gear stick quite quickly, the same applied, so it did not take long for me to cotton on what not to do. After a few lessons, she declared I was fit to take the driving test with the words:

"My reputation is in your hands so if you dare to fail, there will be no more lessons from me!"

Then came the day of the test we were sat in the waiting room as this not very happy chappy came in "Your name Pritchard?". I managed to squeak "yes". No preamble; it was out to the car, "just follow my instructions". These were left, right three-point turn as it was called in those days, reverse turn when I smack my hand on this book stop. As I was travelling along, a coal wagon came out in front of us a little quick, discharging a sack of coal right in front of us, I slammed the brake on, and he nearly went through the window, so no other emergency stop was required.

At this point, we made our way back to the depot. When we stopped, my sphincter muscles decided to relax, so the poor fellow did the paperwork out in double quick time so he was able to exit the car into some fresh air plus I had passed, so I dare face my instructor with a smile.

THE GARAGE

Working in a garage led us to have a course of do's and don'ts relating to road awareness. Being ten mile away, we travelled by car, normally a Ford V8 Pilot, a large motor that was more than big enough to transport us all. One week the Ford was in disgrace, needing repair work. Our other option was a two-seater Triumph sports car. By the time we all squashed in, the only seat with any comfort was the drivers. Would you believe this was the week they discussed? Overloading of vehicles, any type of vehicle, oops.

While heading for the double gates to let us out of the compound, a policeman was wishing everyone good-night, the only thing in our favour it was dark. Our driver insisting we kept still and very quiet, "no problem", say we. Arriving opposite the policeman, he said goodnight, as in chorus we said "goodnight, goodnight, goodnight, and goodnight". We did not see the policeman's reaction, as the car's exhaust hit the road, showering sparks everywhere as we screamed out of the yard. The driver mentioned something about it being a very silly thing to do, or at least that is what he was trying to say in between expletives. But it is a normal reaction when someone says goodnight, isn't it?

I was one of those young men who possessed an unruly head of hair. One day while taking a car out on test I happened by the barbers shop, and noticing it was empty, I popped in for a haircut they used to be called a short back and sides, this normally took no more than three minutes. On my return back to the garage, as I parked the car, the foreman was striding out in my direction. He walked around me a couple of times then commented:

"You have had your hair cut!" (You could not miss it).

I could not deny it, so I said "Yes."

"You have had it cut in the firm's time!"

"Yes," I said, "it grows in the firms time."

He glared at me and said,

"It does not all grow in the firm's time"

I replied, "I did not have it all off!"

This warranted a march to the manager's office. I thought this is it, bye-bye to my apprenticeship. I felt I was standing to attention in front of the manager while the foreman related the story. The manager cracked out laughing and told me to get back to work, 'you cheeky so and so'. It took a while for the foreman to come to terms with what had happened. I had to be on my best behaviour for quite a while.

With being in an apprenticeship, you had to spend time in each department, and this is how I finished up with Albert, now Albert was in the tank regiment in the war, unlike many others who stayed very quiet about the goings-on, with him, it was *put your tin hats on I will tell you a war story* (not again) my goodness.

Albert was in charge of the body shop, panel beating, spraying and so forth. A customer came in on one occasion with a water leak in the boot. These were often difficult to find as water tracked from one area to another. After a while, having no luck, Albert said, "I will climb into the boot with a torch while you play water over it with a hosepipe. While doing this, I saw the customer coming for his car, so I put the hosepipe down.

"Is the car ready?" He says,

"Oh yes."

So he jumped in and drove off Soon after he thought he had developed a puncture. On stopping and looking around his car, he noticed a noise in the boot.

As he opened it Albert popped out, and begged a lift back to the garage. I heard him return from a distance yelling:

"Where is he? Where is he? I will ring his b.....y neck when I catch him."

As you can imagine, I kept well out of his way for quite a while; however, next time someone came in with a leak, guess who finished up in the boot.

Two people had to stay on an hour later on a rotation system to cover any breakdowns and put any vehicles away, either in the garage or around the back. Notes were often put on, like 'be careful with the brakes', or 'the steering is dodgy'. This particular evening, while it was my turn on the late shift, a rather large lorry had to be parked around the back facing a wall, no problem taking it round, however, when I stopped I was unable to stop the engine. I tried the key – nothing; I looked all over for the full stop, with no luck. So I went looking for my partner, for advice, no he did not know either. I could not leave the engine running all night, so I put it in first gear, put my foot firmly on the brake and slowly let the clutch out, hoping to stall the engine. The lorry kept rocking away, touching the wall in front of it; just as the engine died, a section of the wall fell into the river; oh my goodness, I had a very restless night. I had to face the consequences the next morning. I decided to go into work early; it appears the person who had booked the vehicle in had not put a note in explaining the pull stop had broken off, so I did not take all the blame. The wall finished up as an insurance job. And the lorry was no worse for wear.

At one time I used to work in the garage during the day; I then travelled across the city to a petrol station that belonged to the boss, where I took over serving petrol from the day staff for extra a bit of extra money. This was also the time I was able to do repairs to my own car in between serving customers.

On one occasion I had quite a serious repair to carry out, as I had realised during the day that my brakes were not performing as they should. So buying all the spares I required I set off to travel across the city. It was during this trip that things went, what you would describe, as very unfortunate with the brake pedal going straight to the floor when I tried to stop. Fortunately I managed to stop by using the hand brake.

Thing went from bad to worse as I travelled up the Headrow in Leeds when trying to stop at the first set of traffic lights my hand brake cable broke. In those days most cars had bumper bars – I had no option but try mine out; fortunately the car in front had a bumper the same height as mine. The good thing was we were going uphill at the time so it was not such a big bump. The driver did look round with a bemused look on his face.

Would you believe the next traffic lights were also at red the same thing happened, he did not bother to look round this time, his door shot open and he was next to my window in no time at all saying things like what the b-l you think you are playing at, I sat there very sheepish trying to explain my predicament, all the while trying my hardest to balance the accelerator and the clutch to prevent me from rolling backward. During this tirade he noticed the new brake shoes and fittings on my back seat.

He said, "What! What! those feking things should be on your wheels not lounging about on your back seat, where are you hoping to go in that state?"

"I am trying to get across the city to Burly Road" I replied.

"Well" he said "It looks like I had better stay in front of you until you get there, hadn't I? Just try your best to hit me as gentle as you can."

That's how I made my destination. I was very glad it was not a policeman in front of me.

We used to have to test cars out for performance. This particular car was an old Citroën – the one with the gearbox at the front. Our test road was a straight mile with a very sharp bend at the end.

I set off in this motor picking up speed as I went. Just as I came toward the end of the mile I applied the brakes ... or so I thought! Apart from a funny feeling, on looking out of the rear view mirror I noticed a stream of what could only be brake fluid making its way out from under the car.

Knowing the car had no chance of slowing down let alone stopping I sat there seeing the corner coming up at a rate of knots, I thought, "don't just sit there panic!" I think I took the corner on what I thought was one wheel as it was doing all sorts of acrobatics before cruising to rest in the middle of the road. Luckily for me there were no other vehicles on the road at that time. I went back to the garage at a very sedate pace, still shaking and feeling very sick, but so lucky to come out of it in one piece.

MARGARET WILSON

Margaret worked in the office with a couple of other girls; she was a little older than me, and we appeared to get along quite well. Then one day, she asked if I would take her out, which I agreed to do. The date was arranged for the next evening which came and went. When I arrived at work the next morning, George came to me and said, "Were you supposed to take Margaret out last night?" (Oh, my giddy aunt). George went on to say, "I went past on the bus, and Margaret was waiting at the bus stop, what's more, when I returned home, she was still at the bus stop, so if I were you I would make myself very scarce for at least a week". Needless to say, she never spoke to me again—what a thing to forget.

Generally, I was not one for playing fast and loose; however, on one occasion, I had been going out with a girl, and I thought we had broken up. I went on my merry way and started going out with another girl until one evening I was speaking to this girl at the front step when mum told me the other girl was wishing to speak to me at the back door. Would you believe they both took off in a hurry saying,

"We will remember this" ... not a good night's sleep that night.

Deidre came storming into the garage shouting:

"Who owns the big silver car outside?" she waited until a guy came out of the office

"It's mine, Do you not know who I am?"

"Er no"

"I am Matt Munro!!"

"I could not give monkeys if you're Marilyn Monroe your cars still blocking my forecourt".

BREAKDOWN TRUCK

This vehicle was an eight cylinder petrol engine, only in winter it was a pig to start, the colder the conditions the worse it was. It was hired out to the local council in winter with a snow plough attached. It had to be out of the yard by 5am. The guy called James who was allocated to drive it had just left the army and he was larger than life. It was his job to get this truck started at that time by any means available to him including lighting a small fire underneath the engine (who mentioned anything about health and safety?) So this fire would warm the oil for it to flow more freely and make it easier to start. This and a starting handle (for those not familiar with a starting handle, it was a device that slotted into the front of the engine and the operator had to turn the engine manually hence saving on battery power). There could be drawbacks with this method as occasionally the engine could backfire meaning this handle would turn in the opposite direction at a very quick speed and if the handle was not held properly it meant a dislocated thumb or worse.

Once it sprang into life James would celebrate by giving the loudest rendition you have ever heard of *Rose Marie*, (his pet name for the truck), this while throwing the starting handle in the air. This normally would not matter only the foreman lived in the cottage next to where the truck was parked up! Not being thrilled to bits about being roused at that unearthly hour of the morning.

I am unable to say what names James was called, whatever it was it was like water off a duck's back as next time the truck started up the whole sequence was repeated. At a more conducive time for people to emerge still in cold weather the truck was reluctant to start.

Another method was to use ether. Someone (usually a young person) would sit on the truck front wing holding this over the air inlet. Not having the provisions we have today our method was to have a rag dipped in ether obtained from a friendly chemist nearby. On one occasion the truck started just as the young person slid off the wing into a very sound sleep, the wind must have been in the wrong direction on that day blowing toward him. Just in the way of explanation ether was the same product hospitals and dentists used to help put a patient to sleep prior to an operation, it had the opposite effect on our truck and it helped us to get it started.

The time came for me to take control of the breakdown wagon (scary).

My first job was to go to a local quarry to remove a dynamo from a shed. No one told me this item was 40ft down inside a big hole, and they had removed the roof of the shed in which the thing was in! All I had to do was back up over the first railway line and very carefully edge to the next line, by which time the jib was hanging over the hole.

Letting the cable out until it reached the dynamo, all the information was relayed between a man who stood at the back of the truck and me, and people down below. The people below connected the hook on my cable to the dynamo, then relayed the information for me to start winding the cable in. It was stuck, wasn't it, so the jib at the rear of the tipped backwards, meaning my cab lifted up – ooh crickey – there is me leaning forward trying to hold the cab down (fat chance).

The thing at the end suddenly released, dropping the cab down very quickly. After it stopped bouncing up and down I gingerly began to raise the dynamo, I think the weight of it was about as much as my engine would take; so there I was sweating at the controls trying my utmost to lift it out of the quarry – that was until the thing on the end started swinging from side to side – meaning the front of the truck was moving left and right. By that time, I nearly did a very childish thing. After what seemed an eternity, it finally reached the top. All I had to do now was move forward, that was until I got to the second railway line, backward and forward a few time. I was rewarded with a climb over the line. It was just a case now of placing it onto a waiting lorry. All I had to think about was doing it all over again after it had been serviced.

TREE STUMPS

The breakdown truck was hired out to the local council to help with some jobs deemed too difficult for them to undertake, one of these included removing tree stumps once the tree had been cut down and removed.

The idea was for us to pull the stump out easy-peasy not on your nelly, the workers said *you just (that word) put the cable around the stump and drag it out*, bearing in mind our breakdown truck was a hefty beast you would think everything should go to plan. Let the cable out then fasten it around the stump, start pulling. What you do not expect is the stump stayed where it was and the truck starts moving backward, so all we have to do is put a couple of stout wedges behind the wheels and try again, so into to winch gear and gently let the clutch out. After

climbing over the wedges we realised there was going to have to be a plan three. It should be just a case of digging a bit more soil out from around it.

One hour later we tried again, as before fastened the cable around the trunk and so on, plenty of revs for the power we needed, let the clutch out slowly. There was such a horrendous bang as the very thick bowden cable broke, it lashed up toward the cab hitting the roof dead centre causing a 6"(15cm) dent and breaking the windscreen. Had it been a few inches to my side it would have been curtains for me or anyone else in its way. I staggered out of the cab shaking like a leaf, up until that time I did not realise I had a stutter.

ANOTHER COUNCIL JOB

The highways department decided they would widen the road next to the town hall, the only problem was there were two very big sandstone gate pillars to move.

A gang of men were employed to dig an area around the pillars and a two metre trench behind them. I arrived for a look see. I thought *they are going to be very, very heavy.*

Next the road was cordoned off for me to get into position, I now placed the jib over the pillar and a chain was placed quite low down on the pillar, I then attempted to raise it off the ground. Winch gear on, rev's on, foot gently off the clutch – that is until the back of the truck decided it wanted to sit down. The only problem was when it was lifted it had to be moved back for two metres.

I decided I needed to go back to the workshop and find something suitable and very heavy to attach to the front to try and compensate. After much looking I found two very heavy water jacks. These were placed on the front bumper where it fastened to the chassis.

Off we go again, this time it just allowed me to lift the gate stoops enough to very slowly move backward. Once in position I released the winch brake. I did not have to ask it to lower.

A couple of weeks later I was asked to go back and do the same with the second one. I forgot to say with all the noise in the cab and unable to see what was going on behind, there had to be one man stood next to the cab door and another behind the truck to relay messages.

After lifting the stoop and moving it back to the new position the winch brake released easing all the weight of the truck, at which time all hell broke loose shouting me to lift the stoop back up.

As you can imagine the mechanics in the cab took a little while to get around getting it lifted off the ground. This when I was told a workman had his hand under the stoop when it fell. Jumping out of the cab to see state this guy was in, (considering two ton of sandstone had just crushed his hand and the lower part of his arm) he was in far better spirits than me, apart from me ready to pass out, realising what I had just done.

The foreman put him in his car and took him to hospital. Apparently he had noticed a lump under the stoop and tried to brush it away. Considering the weight of this thing I do not think it would have made any difference.

I had to go straight home and try to come to terms with what had happened. I was in a bit of a state for a few days.

Atfer I'd gone back to work for a few days the injured man came in to see me, with his arm in a sling, being a young man I found it very nerve-wracking facing him. He on the other hand was quite matter of fact about it. Telling me he would be on light duties when he returned to work and been paid for all the time he was off.

It was shortly after this period I decided to move to another type of work. I went for an interview as a milking machine fitter.

The interview went as follows:

"Can you walk?"

"Yes."

"Can you drive?"

"Yes".

"You're hired!"

Now it may have had something to do with my engineering background, or they were desperate for fitters.

I returned home to explain to my wife I had found another job with a £4 a week cut in pay, you can imagine she was not impressed. However I soon made the £4 back and more beside.

A NEW CHAPTER

The dairy industry had for some time been undergoing a transformation, from hand milking to machine milking. Dairy herds were increasing in size, hence the need for more sophisticated and quicker milking methods were needed.

The installation of this equipment and machinery was such that the time taken could and often did run into weeks rather than days. It was necessary for the fitter to stay on the farm. This aspect was often built into the contract.

NIP AND POP

There are managers who think of their men, there are managers who think of their customer, and there are those who like the quiet life. William Storm was of the latter breed.

My first introduction to William was at the interview for the position of 'milking machine engineer mentioned on the previous page.

I hadn't realised they were so desperate for fitters. The fact that I was a qualified mechanical engineer might have helped somewhat.

During my interview, the telephone rang. The conversation, as I understood it, was with a very irate farmer asking when his installation was going to be fitted.

"It will not be long, sir." Cough. "We have another fitter starting soon, in fact, right away!"

I sat there thinking - he can't mean me! What about training? But he did, and that is how I came to be in this situation.

After intensive training, needing the absorption capacity of a sponge, slight of hand quicker than Paul Daniels, the flexibility of a gymnast and the stamina of an ox, and they were just the easy bits! Six months of training condensed into six weeks.

During those early days of introducing mechanisation to the dairy farming world, there was just not enough qualified fitters - the people who could make a farmer's dreams come true or turn them into nightmares.

These were the boom days of the 1950s and 60s. Farmers began to see the advantages of engineering technology in farming. It gave them 'hands-off' milking.

As mentioned, the company I was about to work for certainly did not have enough fitters, installers, call us what you will. There was just not enough of us to meet the demand. William's role as manager was to programme the team's installation work and provide job sheets so that we knew where we were going. More important, the type of installation involved. This was usually a pipeline for thirty-six cows etc. or a free-standing milking parlour.

No mention of installation details were given. This always appeared to be a secret. The revelation unfolded after arriving on-site and looking around.

Later in my career, this was brought home to me when arriving on a farm. Still sitting in my van, I was asked by the farmer, "It's taken thee long enough to get here. How long is it going to take thee to do the job?"

Not knowing what I was up against, building-wise, then realising they were old stone walls.

Tongue in cheek, I said, "I'll look round for a couple of days and weigh the job up, then make a start."

With a look of horror, he turned around and shot off up the three steps to the front door shouting: "Ada, Ada, there's a bugger here going to look round for two days before he gets a set-off!"

This was not quite the case, and the job went smoothly once the farmer had calmed down and we looked at the work involved!

On the other side of the coin, the side we did not always see, William was responsible for customer relations. It was his job to keep the customer happy and, so we thought, pave the way in readiness for the day we arrived on site. In reality, William operated on the premise that; "he who shouts loudest gets the best attention". His understatements and attempts at keeping faith with the farmers led to his nickname of 'Nip and Pop'.

He was prone to sending us all over the country at a minute's notice. He would call us into his office at the company headquarters in Cheshire, to check the job sheets, pinned on the wall in order of priority, "loudest soonest".

Each of us had a preference as to which part of the country in which we wished to work, Cheshire being bottom of the list. Not to besmirch the Cheshire farmer, this being considered home territory, did not qualify for the lucrative sixpence (6d) an hour extra for being away from home.

It was the company's custom to take a 10 percent deposit with each order to induce loyalty from the customer and keep the opposition at bay. This arrangement often generated abuse and threats of legal action, considering it may have been at least a calendar month between paying the salesman and clapping eyes on the fitter. Alternatively, William would be sat there shuffling papers, probably nothing to do with the job which we were about to go on, look up, then very politely say, "Would you mind nipping over to Sunderland and pop in a bit of milking equipment for Mr So and So" (name and address supplied).

This was said in a manner which, to the unsuspecting, might suggest a ten-minute job at the end of the road. No such luck. Invariably it meant something like a six-hour drive followed by several days hard graft.

I was now beginning to understand that the company was well behind the promised starting dates for all the jobs on their books. Unbeknown to us, excuses were made on our behalf. The word 'our' did not refer to the company, as you may think, but to us, the fitters given the task of installing the company's equipment.

William's promises and excuses went beyond the bounds of a mere mortal's imagination. In those early days, we would arrive on site to be greeted with comments like, "How's your broken leg? See, you've got the plaster off then; how did you do it?"

"Who? Me? I'd rather not say," would be the reply.

Not surprising since it was the first time I, or any of my fellow fitters, would have heard of the terrible tragedy which had befallen us in the previous weeks. We didn't even know which leg we had injured or the extent of the damage sustained. It was better to say nothing.

Looking back, we must have had more broken legs on the team than any football club. In no time at all, we became adept at not showing surprise at such comments. After all, when you have had one broken leg! I very quickly acquired the knack of appeasing my agricultural acquaintances and began developing my perverse sense of humour, this was probably called survival!

The practice of the company was whoever started an installation finished it, barring death or accident. Remembering my very first encounter on a farm during training, this particular fitter I went with was known as 'Tommy the Terrible'. Tommy, believing he had completed the previous job, appeared surprised when told that Mr Ferguson had been on the phone. Mr Ferguson was not impressed with the work done and demanded satisfaction. Said William, "You had better go back and take Ron with you." As we entered the farmyard, the farmer must have seen and recognised the van. He was stood waiting for us, with a shotgun, shouting; "If that so called fitter gets out I'll let him have both barrels."

First farm visit, what have I let myself in for?

I crept out of the van with my hands up, stammering words like "Would you like to tell me what the problem is sir?" (Me being absolutely clueless as to the workings of said piece of machinery). "What's wrong with it sir?"

"What's wrong with it, what's bloody right with it! Come and have a look for yourself. Would you accept a job like this?"

I had to admit even to the untrained eye it was less than perfect, in fact it was atrocious.

Talking the farmer into letting Tommy escape from the vehicle wasn't easy. I had to promise that together we would sort it out. This took exactly twice a long as starting from scratch. After receiving the farmer's seal of approval, we both departed very relieved.

Our illustrious manager sent me to a farm near Egremont, in Cumberland, now Cumbria. "The stall work is on site Ron, so would you mind nipping up to Cumberland and popping it in."

It's a long drive from Cheshire to the West Coast of Cumberland, where the farm was situated. I arrived at the farm in the middle of dinner. The farmer was far from amused at being called away from his meal to answer the door. I received a tirade of abuse, and a liberal spray of chewed food, also a cursing which seemed to last forever. "It's about time your company invested in some decent vehicles."

To my knowledge there had been nothing wrong with the vehicles. William strikes again. Thanks Bill. But even farmers pause for breath occasionally.

When he eventually eased off, I said "Shall I go out and come back in again, or shall I go out and stay out?"

The response was; "Ah suppose thou's hungry, thou'd better sit down and have some dinner."

All I could manage to squeak was; "No thanks, don't feel very hungry at the moment, thank you."

On the completion of the job, we parted on good terms.

NEW FANGLED CONTRAPTIONS

It wasn't all dirty fingernails and sore heads being a milking machine fitter in the dairy industry. The early mornings, cold bedrooms and cow muck were only part of the job. There were lighter moments from time to time.

On one occasion I was sent out to a farm in the Derbyshire countryside to install a milk pipeline, which was my forte in those days. The farmer, I'll call him Henry for this little story, was of the old school. There was no electricity on the farm, nor was there any machinery to speak of.

He had no tractor, no milking machinery, in fact the only piece of machinery Henry had on the farm was a brand new three-hp petrol engine, bought by Henry. This was to drive the vacuum pump I was about to install, along with a galvanised vacuum pipeline around the cowshed. This was a vacuum line to the mechanical milking machine buckets, used for drawing milk off the cow.

The fact that there was an engineer on the farm - me - had a dramatic effect on Henry. Whilst I was there he decided this was a good time to modernise. He would get a tractor! Not only that, he would install a water closet to replace the old 'thunderbox', which required frequent emptying.

"Thou'll come in handy for doin' the pipework, seein' tha's got tackle."

Something of an opportunist was our Henry!

The farm was on a hill so a tractor would be a definite advantage for Henry, if only to take the churns of milk from the farm, down the lane to the bottom of the hill, where the dairy collection point was. From there they would be taken by the milk marketing board truck to the dairy, a task that normally took about one and a half-hours by his horse and cart. I had often seen him standing on the back of the cart, reins hanging loose, whilst his knackered old horse, way beyond retirement age, picked its way slowly and deliberately down the lane, with Henry surveying his fields "Doing his farming!"

I drove him into the nearby town and helped him to organise a provisional driving licence and complete the usual formalities.

The new tractor, a grey Ferguson, arrived and stood in the farmyard gleaming whilst Henry eyed it up like a child with a new toy. We eventually 'nailed' a pair of 'L' plates on, and Henry loaded his milk-laden churns into the back box. I stood back to watch him drive off - no - first he would; "go into the house and put summat on to keep t'wind out, tractor's going to be a bit faster than t'hoss."

When he reappeared he was wearing what looked like all the clothes he owned, topped off with cap and scarf. Talk about Nanook of the North!

"Expecting bad weather Henry?"

The comment was received with a grunt. Henry climbed onto his new tractor, stood up, had a good look round, he started the engine and lurched out of the farmyard to deliver his milk. I went back to the task in hand, installing the milk pipeline.

Some two hours later I realised that I had not seen Henry return from his excursion. Consternation grew when after two and a half-hours he still had not returned. The task only took an hour and a half with the horse and cart, it should have been quicker by tractor. It didn't take me much longer to decide that it might be a good idea to go and look for him. I set off down the lane to find him, following the route I knew he would take, half expecting to find him parked on the grass verge; "Doing his farming."

I continued down the hill until I reached the T-junction at the end of the lane, and there it was, Henry's brand new tractor, in the ditch with milk and churns all over the place. Oh, Henry, he was sitting on the banking just looking at the whole sorry mess.

I leaped out of the van shouting "What on earth's happened?"

As I mentioned before, Henry was in the habit of letting the horse walk down the lane unaided whilst he stood up and took stock of his fields.

Henry looked up and said; "As I got towards t'end of lane, I stood up, pulled on the steering wheel and shouted 'WHOA'! The blinking thing shot across t'road and in't ditch. Bloody new fangled thing, I'll use t'hoss tomorrow." He did, I never saw him on the tractor again after that day.

You will recall that Henry was a born and bred opportunist, once he had recovered from the tractor incident he was soon back on form. The water closet became his next priority. Henry worked with a will, calling on me from time to time to lend a hand with the pipe work. "We" piped up the water from the farmhouse to the point where it would be connected to the cistern, and Henry worked on happily, leaving me to get on with the task of installing the milk pipeline. It seemed that Henry was no longer interested with the progress in this area. The new toilet block was his main priority. All continued well until sometime later whilst working in the shippon I had to go to the van to pick up a piece of equipment. I had almost reached the van when I thought I heard a cry of some sort. It didn't really register so I continued to the van, picked up the item I wanted and went back to carry on with the job. Later I had to go to the van once again, and the same thing happened. There was the muffled sound of someone shouting for help, if a faint sound can be described as a shout. Considerable time had passed since I last heard it, so I thought I should investigate. The sound appeared to come from the new WC, which now had its door fitted. The door was closed. But the cry for help definitely came from within.

"You all right?" I shouted through the door.

"No I'm bloody well not," said the feeble voice, "Open the door will you?"

"Right," I said. "Stand back."

"I can't," came the reply.

"But the door opens inwards," I said.

"Then rip it off!" replied the strained voice.

That's going to be easier said than done I thought. I gave the handle a bit of a tug, nothing much happened.

"Hurry up will you," said Henry.

I gave it another tug a bit harder this time, no joy. The only option was to take it off the hinges, a screw driver job.

Eventually after taking out most of the screws, the door flew off, rapidly followed by the upper half of Henry coming out backwards and lay on the floor by my feet. The rest of him appeared to be disappearing down the toilet bowl.

"What the!" Henry was covered in porcelain pieces of cistern, like bits of jigsaw puzzle. Once he had regained his composure, a state quickly achieved by the use of a stream of the most colourful words I had ever heard, and some, which I had not come across until that day.

In his enthusiasm to bring his new WC into service, Henry would install the cistern in readiness for me to pipe up. You may not be aware dear reader that in those days it was deemed necessary to mount the cistern at a height, which would endanger low flying aircraft. This was to ensure sufficient water velocity to flush away all traces of whatever happened to be in the pan. This required the cistern to be lifted up and onto the brackets several feet from the floor. To do this Henry stood with one foot on each side of the top of the bowl, and tried to lift the cistern in place. All went well until at the very last moment of 'the lift' when the wayward cistern caught itself prematurely on one of the support brackets, knocking Henry off balance. Both feet shot down the pan, the cistern fell and smashed to smithereens, filling the said pan, Henry fell backwards securely wedging himself against the door. He was not going anywhere without the cavalry.

By now the milk pipeline installation was almost complete, all that was required was for the pump to be installed then the system could be commissioned and Henry would be free from handling milk forever. The pump was to be driven by a three horsepower petrol engine, mentioned earlier, which Henry had provided. He had also constructed a concrete bed to which he had bolted the engine down. The pump was installed and connected to the engine by vee-belts. A drop of petrol in the tank and we were ready for a trial run. Henry was in good spirits and raring to witness the start up. I checked the vee-belts for tension, and ran through the starting procedure for Henrys benefit, as this would be his job in future. I then started the engine for a trial run. The engine burst into life and immediately leaped into the air like some demented March hare. This being due to Henry's poor cement mix. The only restraint, which stopped it from escaping out of the farmyard and down the road, was the vee-belt drive.

"You going t'stop it Ron?"

"No, you are Henry!"

The engine was leaping about like something possessed. "We'll wait for it to run out of petrol, or seize up."

In the fullness of time it stopped. It was later re-installed on a substantial bed of sand and cement where it did perform for many years.

Once a mechanical milking system was installed on a farm it was usual to train every farmer who had previously hand milked, in the use of the equipment, and also how best to introduce it to his cows. Unlike hand milking, there is a considerable amount of noise generated by mechanical milking systems. The clanking of metal on metal, the hissing of air, a multitude of sounds, all of which can make a cow very, very nervous. The farmer, being calm and relaxed and knowing how to handle his stock is an important asset at this stage.

Once the cow is in position for milking, the general procedure is to stand alongside, place a shoulder well into the beast's groin, and push hard. The effect of this is to partially move the animal off balance and thus prevent it from kicking. At the first milking I'd demonstrate the technique to the farmer.

Taking four or five minutes with each beast, to make sure that he understands. Invariably the farmer's turn always came at the same time his favourite cow appears. Henry was no exception. The favourite cow appeared as if by magic in time for his first attempt. Like many farmers before him, Henry thought he knew his cattle well, enough for them to accept anything he did. The result was he did not get close enough to the animal to achieve the desired effect. Offering up the milking cluster to the beast, which had never experienced the like before, caused it to promptly lash out with half a ton of hind leg, in a scything motion. The milking cluster, false teeth, specs and Henry went in different directions, upwards, outwards, backwards, downwards, in that order. The favourite cow was no longer the pride of Henrys life. And his comments regarding the bloody new fangled equipment and the poor animal are not repeatable. Henry dragged himself to his feet and disappeared into the house never to be seen again. I wonder if he ever did get the hang of it!

FARMHOUSE FARE

As you can imagine, staying away from home for long periods meant that there was no going home for a spot of lunch or an evening meal.

Nevertheless, the need to eat was there, the job lent itself to generating hunger.

First and foremost, there was no point asking for a menu, you worked on the basis they all look fit and healthy, you ate with them and you ate what they ate, or not at all.

I remember one of the meals early in my career, which happened to be tea, on a farm in Leicestershire. All the milk produced on the farm was used to make various cheeses, Red Leicester by the tonne. You knew you were getting near the place from about three miles away, down wind. I could have found it blindfold!

We, that is the family and myself, sat around a typical farm dining table with numerous cheeses set in containers down the middle. Granddad reached over, took the lid off one cheese, it appeared to shoot across the table to him, promptly followed by THE SMELL, which when released from the confines of its sealed contained, cloaked everything in the room with a very strong aroma.

I remember him saying; "If it doesn't move, it isn't worth eating."

Only cheese for tea! Not being a cheese fan, you can imagine my popularity when I asked, "Do you have any jam?"

I quickly learned why all farmers had very flexible table knives. After finishing the main course at dinner, this very essential and versatile utensil was used to chase up all the gravy which was then licked off, seconds before the rice pudding appeared in the middle of the plate. Slow learning left me sat there with a quarter of an inch of gravy surrounding the rice pudding, it looked very pretty. It just took a bit of getting down.

Breakfast often started with porridge being eaten out of a small pudding bowl, the same principle as the flexible knife applied, I must try to make a good job of cleaning the bowl, as it would be filled with tea as soon as it remotely resembled empty! A clean bowl had less floating bits in it!

One got used to 'first in best fed'. I was, however, caught with egg on my face at a farm I was visiting for the first time. I don't know why I mentioned that, they were all first timers in those days. I learned fast, and made sure I was first down for dinner. The table was set and laden with piping hot farmhouse fare. I popped a very hot roast potato in my mouth. Was it hot? There I was huffing and puffing as the rest of the family took their places with father solemnly standing at the head of the table, he looked at me and said; "We will now say Grace". Oh no!

One time the lady of the house walking around the table dishing out the dinner.

I'm asked; "do you like potatoes?"

"Yes please."

"Do you like meat?"

"Yes please."

"Would you like one or two beans?"

"Two, please."

She hit me with the pan.

Working in what used to be Cumberland took some getting used to. Big lads are the Cumberland farmers, not surprising. They used to have five meals a day and a bit of supper. I'm sure I spent more time at the table than working!

I have been know to supply part of the main course, but in an unexpected way. Whilst working on one farm I had the need to walk round the dairy in order to connect up the pipes to a pump situated in a small building. Each time I turned the corner the farmer's pet cockerel would appear. Talons outstretched in front, ready for action, it would always be about four feet off the ground flying horizontally and towards me! I warded this bird off in various ways. Jumping with fright every time I turned the corner. I mentioned this to the farmer and asked if he would keep this projectile safely locked up until I had finished my work. This did not happen.

One time, walking round the corner carrying a very large spanner, there it was - the cockerel - in full flight! Warding it off with a back hander it stopped it in mid air. I must have caught it just right, it fell instantly to the ground, to my surprise, stone dead. I picked it up by the feet and carrying it behind my back, walked up and knocked on the front door. The farmer's wife answered.

I said; "What's for dinner tomorrow?"

"Why?" she replied.

I then showed her the deceased bird.

"Oh my goodness what's he going to say?"

We did have chicken for dinner that week, the farmer never said a word.

I was rudely awakened one morning by the sound of a hen cackling - no, not outside - it was laying an egg on my blanket. Talk about breakfast in bed!

Once, while travelling along a narrow country lane, a pheasant attempted a chicken run across the front of my pick-up van. I won, or so I thought. After picking up the bird from the road, I dropped it into the passenger side. Ten minutes later this dastardly beast decided it had been asleep long enough. It didn't just wake up , it did a superb imitation of a Harrier Jump Jet - vertical, horizontal, sideways, wings and feathers everywhere. And I thought it was uncomfortable having a bee in the cab! I had the door open PDQ and set the pesky bird free.

Nothing ever really died on farms. In my early days, if a hen happened to be tottering about, I guarantee that before the end of the week we would have chicken for dinner. I once overheard a family talking about a particular pig being off its food, yes you've guessed, no sooner said than done! A blossom of hams appeared, hung from hooks in the back kitchen, joints cut up and salted ready for future use. On one farm I was working I overheard a conversation referring to Grandmother's health. I didn't stay there long!!

After a hard days work supper was always a welcome event. This was often a smaller version of the cooked dinner. A particular supper in North Lancashire went down quite well.

Afterwards the farmer in the way of conversation said; "How did you enjoy your squiggles?"

I replied; "Very nice, thank you - my what?"

He explained they had been castrating some lambs earlier in the day, and I had just eaten some of the left overs. I managed to keep it down, even though feeling more than a little queasy.

In order to supplement a diet of grass, cows are fed 'feed nuts' known as cow cake. This is often given at milking time having a twofold benefit. First, it placates the beast who thinks it's a reward and secondly, it provides additional vitamins, which produces more milk. Sometimes a scoop is used to roughly measure out an amount fed to the animal. One farmer, with an eye on margins concerning concentrates, used what can only be described as shop scales to give the exact amount, adding a few, taking a few off. This would go on for ages.

On passing him one of these times I said; "Can I have a quarter of those while you are on with it, please?"

All I got was a very surly look.

"Waste not want not," or "It might come in handy some time," entered into every aspect of the farming families life. This being the only household I was served brains, in the form of a 'spreadish', we in ordinary life call it brawn or potted meat. But in its natural state it does look and taste a little different.

Occasionally another fitter would come along to help erect heavy stall-work. We did not always have a choice of who came along to lend a hand. It happened on that this occasion I would take one of our Welsh colleagues, although there wasn't much of him to take to start with. I was soon to find out why when we went in for dinner.

As we sat around the table, the farmer's wife and her daughter kindly dished out the food.

She came to me. "Would you like some beef?"

"Yes please."

My partner - "No thank you."

Next circuit - "Would you like some cabbage?"

"Yes please."

My partner - "No thank you."

Next round - "Would you like some carrots?"

"Yes please".

My ex partner - "No thank you."

How embarrassing.

The lady came round again not a word! A spoon was slammed onto his plate, followed by;

"Everyone likes potatoes." She then quickly walked away.

After this incident, if he was the only fitter available to lend a hand, I would struggle on alone.

A cup of tea was always welcome at any time on farms. "How did I like it?"

"As it comes, wet and warm."

Different types of tea such as China, Indian, Earl Grey etc, were out of place on many farms. This commodity often being bought in bulk from the local agricultural feed merchant. Tea at Mr Purdy's was a taste to behold. An open cauldron hanging from a chain over the fire with soot falling periodically into the water enhanced the flavour. It would not have mattered what type of tea he used, it always tasted the same, smoked, with plenty of body!

SCARECROWS

On rare occasions we would have a leisurely day out, a drive in the country or seaside. These always resulted in a delivery to "Mr So and So's." Sometimes we never got to our original destination. This particular evening was no exception. Having set off dressed in casual clothes, I elected to call in on a local farmer. On our arrival our farming friend was just finishing his day's work and was still smiling over a recent happening, this being part of a long running sequence of events.

Apparently in this part of the country(?) a best-dressed scarecrow competition had been part of the rural scene. Our friend Lew had his scarecrow in a wheat field. Although it started in a standing position, when the shoots were approx three inches high, Lew had crept across during the hours of darkness and knelt it down. Any local farmer passing looking from the road would be amazed at the height of the crop!

He went on to tell us that about 2 am, when he was fast asleep, there was a frantic knock at the door, he trundled downstairs to answer the back door to find two burly officers of the law. "Excuse us sir, is this yours?"

"This" being a body laying in an unnatural angle on the floor.

"Yes", replied Lew.

"I will say this, it has given us quite an eventful time, having received a call from a near hysterical road user. We came out here post haste to find this, er, body with its torso laying in the hedgerow and the legs and feet out into the highway. To say the least giving a passing motorist something of a fright! Obviously a friend of yours must have had the idea this tactic could slow down your chances of winning."

Lew went on to tell my wife and I a similar thing had happened again, with the police awakening him in the early hours. Another of his friendly rivals had removed the Hotel sign board leaving what looked like a gallows and then hung his scarecrow from the cross bar. This time an unsuspecting motorcyclist and his pillion passenger had come around the corner in very wet conditions and their headlamps lighting on this figure hanging from the gallows.

To say he braked suddenly is an understatement. Our storyteller did all the actions, waving his arms about, jumping about in muddy puddles, liberally spraying both of us from head to toe.

On parting, Lew said, "If thou sees someone wearing a top hat, thee let me know, because some one has pinched the one off my scarecrow."

I wasn't sure if my wife enjoyed the impromptu entertainment or substitute for our planned night out, although she did laugh in between dabbing mud from her clothes!

Home James; another night out bites the dust!

AT WORK

Many of you may know cowcake (a strange name for something that comes in a pellet shaped form). In order for it to arrive on the farm from the feed mill it is transported in bulk form on lorries designed to this purpose. An area is set aside on the farm in which to accept this bulk load, this usually being a loft, often above the milking parlour, where it can be fed directly to the cattle during milking. It sometimes works out that the farmer may be away while the cowcake is being delivered, this is not always a problem, because the driver has often been to the farm many times and knows the ropes. The procedure normally followed is that the driver places a large flexible hose into said loft and then blows the contents from the lorry into the space above, he then withdraws the hose and takes off to his next destination.

This works well until, as on this particular occasion, there was a new driver.

On returning home the farmer said to me; "Have the feed firm been?"

I - "Yes they have."

The farmer - "Where the 'L' have they put it?"

I - "As far as I know, in the loft."

Farmer - "Well it isn't there now."

Strange. We soon found out where it was, when the farmer went up to get changed ready to restart work, he was unable to get into his bedroom, yes, you've guessed it - his bedroom was next door to the feed loft and having a broken window in his bedroom didn't help matters at all!! Can you imagine coming home to five ton of small pellets in the place you were expecting to kip? It might have blown in easily enough, it was certainly a different proposition taking it out!

A milk tanker driver is a person that goes from farm to farm collecting the day's milk and transferring it to a dairy to be processed. I think some of them must have been on piecework. We all have our bad days, and here are two little incidents that happened while I was on these particular farms.

A tanker driver came bowling into the farmyard, whips round away from the dairy, into reverse, foot off the clutch and stops in time to see the dairy wall cascading down the rear of the vehicle.

The farmer was not impressed. He got on the telephone. "Is that the milk marketing board etc etc".

Driver leaves premises with a flea in his ear.

About ten minutes later the same driver reappears back in the yard, a much braver man than me, only this time he was going quite a bit slower, probably because he was on foot.

"Is Mr Barnes about," says he.

To which I replied; "Why?"

"I would like to borrow a tractor."

"What for?"

"I've missed the bridge with the tanker and finished up in the stream."

"Oh, I see. Well, I think you will have to ask him yourself"

Telephone again - "Is that the milk marketing board etc etc."

The second event happened while I was standing in a farmer's kitchen discussing equipment, as the milk tanker drew up in the yard. The driver connected the outlet pipe to the farmer's milk tank and withdrew the milk. I happened to look out of the window about the same time as the farmer, this was just in time to see the vehicle moving away still attached to the farmer's milk tank like an umbilical cord.

What breakfast? He was out of the door like a jackrabbit shouting and gesticulating as this corrugated hose became longer and longer until this little milk tank broke loose form its anchorage and tried to force its way through the door, at this stage the hose parted.

"Is that the milk marketing board etc etc?"

The next time I visited this farm, he had a large notice fastened to the dairy door with the words 'NOT TO BE TAKEN EXTERNALLY'.

Occasionally it was possible to take my wife along, this would be when I was delivering most of the equipment ready to start fitting it, possibly the following week, when I would then take the remainder of the fittings and stay to carry out the installation.

My wife and I travelled up country to deliver the large items that were needed, on our arrival we both jumped out of the vehicle and arranged with the farmer where would be the most convenient place to unload. This was sorted and we began taking the equipment off the van. After a little while the farmer took me to one side and said; "Who's the lady?"

"That's my apprentice," I said.

"Oh, but aren't you staying with me next week when you come to fit the job?"

"Yes."

"Well, there's a problem you see. We have only one bedroom. I mean, she's female, and it's a double bed."

I said; "Listen fella, if she wants to become a milking machine engineer, she has to take the rough with the smooth, how do you think I feel about it?"

I turned up the following week on my own. "Flipping heck you had me going for a while then, I see I'll have to keep my eye on you".

On one occasion, I was working away in the dairy, while in a stable opposite, the vet was doing a small operation on a cow, this procedure required sedation. His work completed, the vet packed away his equipment and went on his merry way.

Not long after there was a shuffling noise from the stable. I peered out in time to see this cow attempting to scale the bottom half of the stable door, its actions can be best described as that of a puppy trying to climb a large step, first one leg then the other followed by a back hoof banging away on the inside of the door, until it eventually managed to get a back hoof on top of this door.

When you consider that, unlike a puppy, these animals weigh above half a ton, there is no way you are going to stand there to catch it when it finally gets all its legs over, which it did. Then with an almighty thump it landed on the yard. Now, this beasty was still groggy from the anaesthetic, so no amount of coaxing was going to get it to go anywhere I would wish it to be, instead it staggered across the yard at a fair pace and mounted some stairs, these being only just wide enough for people to climb comfortably, they had a right angled turn which the cow negotiated successfully, hanging over the little platform before turning to continue onward and upward. By the way these steps had no handrail, making this venture even more precarious.

Finding itself in the room above the dairy where it decided to work off the effects of the anaesthetic, with one of its hoofs coming through the ceiling from time to time. Now not being too slow when it comes to self-preservation, it was definitely time to stage left and exit the dairy.

The cow eventually located the way out and descended the stairs in much the same way as it went up, there was me thinking it would never make it, but it did, back down onto Terra Firma. It then ambled across the yard to a patch of grass, put its head down and started eating as if nothing had happened, with me standing there trying to recover, ooh, I could do with a cup of tea!

Early on, some of the tools we used were fairly basic. In order to drill holes in walls, a large electrical drill was used, no hammer or percussion action as available today. It was a case of brute force. This occasionally necessitated a colleague to work with you. The walls on this farm in Cheshire were very, very hard. There I was stood on a pair of steps struggling to hold this drill in line, leaning against the wall with Frank behind pushing me for all he is worth, when all of a sudden this ¾ drill jammed solid, lifting me off my feet with my finger still glued on the trigger, with my arms trying to play themselves and Frank still pushing like a man possessed and my vocal cords trying to scream the words; "Let go and switch the bloody power off".

In a very similar situation, once again I was up the ladder (would I ever learn), the drill bit decided to go through a mains cable. Now, when this happens subsequent events don't take long - on the steps one minute, the next your world goes pear shaped. Apparently after doing a perfect somersault, I landed in the water trough at the back of the dairy. I must admit, pain-wise that's the part I remember most vividly. This was not quite the end of this tale, however. A little while later the farmer's wife came out to find out why her iron had stopped working, even more, the houses in the nearby hamlet had lost their supply, leaving me thinking, I'm lucky to be alive, a few bruises, otherwise okay.

I'd not long arrived on a farm when the son, Barry, came in to where I was working and said; "some of this equipment is German isn't it?"

"Yes. Is there a problem with that?"

"Oh, no it's just that I have a friend called Terry who comes over every night after work to give a hand and I've told him you are German and cannot speak a word of English, and I wondered if you would go along with it for a while?"

"Okay, if I can keep it up, it's going to be difficult mind".

Sure enough, along came Terry, as he did every night. I nodded, he nodded, he then said to Barry; "how to you communicate?"

"He's so used to this type of work, we just use sign language and gestures."

"Yes, but what about food? They eat different food to us don't they?"

"It doesn't seem a problem, whatever we serve up he eats."

Now this deception takes some keeping up, even if it was only in the evenings, because we as a nation have a fascination with foreigners, and Terry was no different to anyone else. He would follow me around everywhere. I would be working away in the workshop with Terry hovering over me, watching every move I made as if I would have different working methods.

After about twenty minutes I said; "Sprechen sie Deutsch?"

"No, no." With that, off he went.

We managed to keep this up for the full week. After loading the van on Friday night, I was in the cab ready to set off when Terry offered me the daily paper. He then quickly withdrew it saying; "I'm sorry pal, I'd forgotten for a minute."

"It's okay Terry," I said. "I've already seen it, thanks all the same".

His jaw dropped, his face was a picture. I left pretty quickly, leaving Barry to explain. After that encounter, word must have got around because every time I worked in that area, farmers called me "the foreigner."

There were times when you really did need a helping hand and this was one of them. It was like trying to get a gallon of water in a pint pot. It was a matter of forcing a hard rubber tube over a much larger stainless steel pipe. This pipe being fitted through a rubber lid. So here we have a lid of approx. 14" across and 2" deep with a 2" pipe sticking out of it. My job was to fit over this pipe a rubber sleeve, the inside diameter of this was about 1".

There never seemed to be an easy way to do this, I would attempt to soften this in hot water, then, placing the lid on the floor, trapped between my knees, I would then try to force this rubber over the pipe. I would just about get the thing on before it decided to escape and dash across the floor with me scooting headlong after it, saying things like; "what a nuisance".

I'd tried many different ways of retaining the lid, like on the floor in the corner of this usually ended up with me scrunched up in a heap, unable to move anywhere. On this occasion, however, help was at hand in the shape of the farmer's daughter.

After seeing my predicament, she offered to lend a hand. She knelt opposite me, holding the lid for grim death against my pushing. Again, at the very last moment, the lid was the victor and we went flying, she backward with me following forward on top of her. That was the first time I'd ever had a soft landing!

At that precise second, the door opened and her father looked in. I must admit it didn't look quite as innocent as it was.

He said; "Oh, I didn't realise you two were at it," and closed the door.

The next time I saw him in the cow shed, I said; "It wasn't what you thought over in the dairy."

"No need to apologise, son. I was young myself once." There was no use trying to explain!

During the winter months, cows are often housed in a building near to the farmyard for a number of reasons. The natural food, grass, doesn't grow in winter, so the animals are at hand to feed, to look after their well being and also for milking. It does have the benefit of allowing the fields to recover and not churned up in inclement weather. It does however, have a downside, that is what to do with all the waste produce, especially since the herds have become much larger.

The waste product has to be stored for up to four months until the frosts firm the soil enough to allow tractors and equipment to travel. In my early days on farms, one of the storage methods was to dig a large pit many metres square approximately one and a half metres deep. As the winter progressed this level of this pit, or lagoon, increased until sometimes it was just about level with the surrounding area, it also formed a crust. This sometimes made it difficult for people new to the farm to know where said lagoon started and finished. Yes, there I was, heading off part of the herd in order to get them into a collecting area, I take a wide berth, straight into the pit! Fortunately it only came up to my armpits. At this stage this product is called slurry or liquid manure, but when you are up to your armpits in the stuff, I hate to say, words such as fertiliser don't really come to mind, it becomes some-thing much more fundamental, like S, H, 1, T!!

Another way of storing the slurry was to build up a wall, again many metres square by approximately two metres high (I don't know why I am using metres, it always used to be in yards, must be something to do with being in the EEC). Anyway, on a cold crisp afternoon, one wall, owing to the pressure having built up behind it, decided to do its interpretation of the Mona dam after the bouncing bomb hit, and eleven tons of slurry took to a nearby road. If you can just imagine this, not a pretty sight. This road was for access only and not used a great deal. Therefore, can you just see the look on the faces of the two dear old ladies in their Morris Minor, as they rounded the corner to be confronted by a wall of not so liquid manure and a farmer's son with a hand-held squeegee saying "hold on a moment, I'll not be long."

If mechanical help had not arrived, he would still be there today. Suffice to say, with health and safety on farms, those days have long gone.

Having the opportunity to work for a Lord was not one to be missed. With equipment prepared and loaded, off I went, best overalls and van washed, lets go. Reaching the stately home in the late evening, there was the elderly housekeeper to greet me with his lordship being away on business. I was shown to my bedroom in order to settle in. These premises were just a touch larger than the average farmhouse. To begin with, there was three staircases, so it was nearly a matter of having a ball of wool in the event of getting lost, you could reel it in and at least get back to your starting point.

On finding my way down into the dining room the next morning, the housekeeper was already waiting for me. "Would you prefer orange or banana for breakfast sir?"

I thought this is a civilised way to start breakfast.

No, this is breakfast.

Now, I know there are people out there who believe this is the way to start the day, but considering my day usually started at eight am and finished somewhere between eight and ten p.m., I should say that being used to an English breakfast, this to me didn't look like a really good substitute!

I was unable to do much about it, so off I went to start work. All the framework had been installed at an earlier date, my part involved fitting the milking equipment to this, such as glass piping, large five gallon Pyrex jars and so forth. Everything was going according to plan until the third day when his lordship returned. He apologised for not being at home when I had arrived, as he had just returned from the House of Lords.

He looked around and said; "Who is the manager on this job?"

"I am."

"Who is the foreman?"

"I am."

"Who is in charge of the job?"

"I am, there is only me here."

He then said; "I am not going to have those bottle things there, I've got some very rough cows and they will not last five minutes."

I said; "I don't think they will be any different to any other cows, that is where we normally put them."

With that he stormed off to phone the company. The company advised him to work out a compromise with me to see how best to site these bottles, ensuring the machine worked efficiently and also protecting the glassware, falling short of his idea, putting them in the loft above. They were lifted and a metal cage put around them. I carried on with the installation with no further interruptions until the day came to test start the equipment.

This day I had a visitor. The test entails circulating water around the plant and making any adjustments necessary. The water is picked up from a trough in the dairy, transported around the glass pipework and bottles, returning into the dairy where it is collected in a large receiving jar, from which it is pumped at high speed back into the wash trough to renew the cycle. The receiving jar holds approximately six gallons, the pump empties this in about twenty seconds through one-inch tube.

When his Lordship sees this, he remarked; "I see what they mean by express dairies."

Very droll.

While it was my job to get the milking machine up and running, there was a local company (who his Lordship held great store by, in fact he said had it been possible they would have fitted the milking equipment). They were installing a device that would transfer the animal feed up into the loft above the milking machine from a large bin in the room next door. This was to be transported using an electric motor turning the screw fixed inside a metal tube. The screw turning slowly would move the feed from one place to the next. I had finished my part, so went next door to see how things were progressing. We were all stood around waiting for the final piece to be completed, this done the start button was pressed. There was a bloody loud bang, everything shuddered and flames belched out of the electric motor.

I said; "Who is the manager on this job?"

His Lordship didn't waste any time phoning their company.

About two to three weeks later, my manager came to me saying; "You remember going to Lord So and So's?"

I said; "Er, yes."

"Well, he has sent a letter to head office stating how pleased he was with the machine and thank the fitter for all his help."

FARMERS' WIVES

Returning home after a week away, the suitcase full of dirty clothes, the unexpected can happen. After plonking the said case on the bed, the catches on the lid flew open, quickly followed by what looked like three weddings worth of confetti.

My wife casually saying; "Oh been to work have you?"

On another occasion, a farmer's wife mentioned as I was leaving; "I noticed your slippers had a hole in them, so I took the liberty of darning them for you."

"Oh, thank you," I replied.

Yes, she darned them lovely with multi-coloured flowers.

My wife asked, "Is that the same place you got married then?"

A farmer friend of mine says; "Ron would not be able to carry out his work if there was no bailer twine available, he seems to string everything up before fixing it in place."

This farm was no exception. I asked the farmer if he had some bailer twine I could use.

"Yes, there's some in the barn around the corner."

So off I went. I had to go past the farmhouse on the way. The farmer's wife, who I would term as cuddly, was kneeling down cleaning the back step and on seeing me remarked; "I haven't time to talk as I'm all behind this morning."

My comment; "I never said a word."

"Cheeky young sod."

I carried on around the corner to find the bailer twine. This usually comes in lengths of about a metre long, where it has been cut off bails and saved. This, however, was the end of a roll, being in the order of sixteen metres. Instead of balling it up, I picked up one end and started walking back, leaving the rest of the twine to trail behind.

On turning the corner the farmer's wife on noticing my return waited until the end of the twine flicked round the end of the wall corner and started laughing, "I hate to upset you but you've lost your dog."

"Dog, I don't have a dog."

"Well, what are you pulling that piece of twine for?"

"Have you tried pushing it?"

"Cheeky young sod."

One well-meaning farmer's wife, living in the North East, did not take any chances with the well being of the people in her care. I could not understand the unusual taste in the drinks which she supplied. One of her sayings was; "Are you alright?" and; "Have you been?" After some detective work, I found that the strange taste in the drinks to be Epsom Salts!

Her strange habits did not end there. One evening she and her friend went off to the cinema. During the performance she handed her friend chocolates. Later in the evening her friend needed to excuse herself in a rush to the toilet. Brynie, that was her name, had only been feeding her friend chocolate laxative!

The poor lady was out of action for a day or two after that. The prank backfired and Brynie found herself with a full time job looking after her needs, and supply reading material slipped under the door, while she was ensconced in the smallest room.

I'm not sure whether she spent time thinking up these fiendish actions or whether they came to her naturally. On one very hot day Brynie's husband was out with the combined harvester cutting the crops. This is one of the most dusty and thirsty jobs imaginable.

Later in the day he called at the farm and popped his head around the door. "Give us a drink lass, I'm gagging."

"There's one waiting for you on the shelf," was the reply.

He strode across the kitchen, picked up the glass and took a long draught, which he immediately sprayed out again.

"Vinegar!" he exploded.

I last heard them hurtling down the passage with him saying things like; "You are a naughty girl."

Brynie and her friend went out for the evening, her husband was off to some local farmers night. I was left holding the fort, no problem. After finishing work then getting washed and changed, I relaxed by laying on the settee watching TV. Normally, you would hear Brynie and friend coming a mile away, but not this evening. The first I knew was when two bodies had launched themselves over the back of the settee. I just about suffocated trying to wriggle out from underneath these two. That's maybe because it took me about ten minutes, when I could have been out in two!

One young feed rep who, in the ladies opinion, had overstepped the acceptable boundaries of good taste, (it was difficult to judge in their case), no by your leave or preamble, they picked him up and unceremoniously dumped him in the horse tough. They then proceeded to find him some dry clothes. I was the nearest size to him. Unfortunately, not having any spare, they robbed Brynie's husband's wardrobe. Well, the poor guy looked like droopy. I couldn't imagine him making any further farm calls that day.

After he had left Brynie said; "I hope his wife is very understanding, she's foreign you know."

A touch of regret, maybe no, I don't think so.

Instead of taking your boots off, most men working on farms find a quiet place to relieve themselves, and so it was with one of the workers in this place. He was in the bullock pen standing at the back, as he thought out of sight, this pen was quite large, holding about a dozen three-quarter grown animals. Little did he know he'd been spotted, that is until our foxy female had picked up a handful of stones and thrown them onto the corrugated room. The startled bullocks set off in a stampede around the enclosure, with the immediate response of our farm hand, caught in mid flow, diving over the nearest barrier. To say I was in their company for about three weeks, I came away fairly unscathed, fer, fer, physically, that is!

COUNTRY ROADS

As you will understand, working in farming and rural communities meant that driving on narrow lanes and roads became an every day event. It was a normal part of country life, and never as stressful as motorway driving. It may not have been so exciting trundling along at a relatively slow speed on roads bounded by walls and hedges. But it did have its moments.

On a lovely evening in high summer I was travelling home and thinking about supper. Driving a medium sized flat fronted van with sliding doors, which were locked in the open position - a bit of ventilation - never amiss on warm summer evenings. Regular driving on minor roads and lanes develops an ability to drive a little faster than perhaps one should. I was heading towards a bend on a particularly narrow piece of road when I saw a car coming towards me from the opposite direction.

We were both going to arrive at the narrowest part at the same time. I slowed down, putting the brakes on quite hard. This set off a chain of events which caused some embarrassment, and a little mirth every time I recall the incident. Behind me in the van, at approximately shoulder height was a shelf, on this shelf was a new one-gallon tin of aluminium paint. This decided to take off, hitting me on the shoulder in its rush to reach Terra Firma. I could not have set up what happened next if I had been a special effects man in the film industry. The tin landed on the road, with its lid facing the car travelling in the opposite direction, the rear wheels of my van ran over it. The lid flew off with the speed of a bullet followed by the quickest mobile spray job you have ever seen. I thought I had better stop, while at the same time cursing my luck at losing a full gallon of paint!

Better try to make light of this event Ron, things could get tricky. Probably not the colour anyone would choose for a two-tone finish. The driver of the other car was not amused, particularly when I took my handkerchief out to clean it off.

Realising that it was hardly adequate, I said; "I'll not be long, going for some rags and cleaner to remove it."

I'm sure he thought that was the last he would see of me. But, true to my word, I returned with a bundle of rags and a tin of turps, borrowed from a nearby farm. Explaining briefly to the farmer my predicament and trying to keep a straight face at the same time.

I set to work to clean off the rest of the paint that my handkerchief had not quite managed to remove. While at this task, the driver elected to get out of the car. That was the first mistake he made, the paint, which was still on the doorsill, transferred itself onto his trouser leg. I didn't like to mention this, being in enough trouble already. I explained that it would be a long time before the underneath of the car would go rusty!

After managing to remove all the silver from the paintwork I was not able to get it off the tyres as the rubber had soaked it in. We parted on fairly friendly terms. He told me that this was the first day of a week's holiday. I met up with him over the course of the week, that is to say, met up with flashes of silver reflecting off the tyres from a distance, because if he saw me first, he turned left, right, or into someone's drive, until I had passed. The evidence remained on that piece of road for about three years.

CALLS OF NATURE

Many of the farms I worked on in the early sixties had outside toilets. It was a real treat to find a water closet, although some left a lot to be desired.

One in particular has the power to bring me out in a cold sweat every time I think about it. The farmer and his wife, who had four teenage daughters, ran this particular farm.

They were a lovely family who welcomed me and made me feel at home from the moment I arrived. It was winter and by the time I arrived late in the afternoon, it was quite dark. The call of nature eventually became necessary, and I was directed to the loo at the end of one of the out buildings in the yard.

Nothing seemed amiss, perfectly normal. In the dark I was lulled into believing that it was just an ordinary loo, in the stark light of day it became a completely different place.

After breakfast, the call of nature had to be answered once again, and I saw this little room in all its splendour. It was tagged on to the end of one of the out buildings, just as it was the night before, some small distance away from the house door. It was alongside a path leading from the house to the garden, which also lead to the barn where the tractors and other farming implements were kept. Not only that, this was the main pathway leading to the road.

The farmer failed to mention that there was no lock on the door, no glass in the window, and a large crack in the cistern, so that when this was about half-full water poured out. It was like sitting under a cold shower. I soon perceived that by pulling the chain on entering allowed a modicum of time before being rudely interrupted by a deluge from above. I saw to my dismay that there was no means of locking the door.

The loo was quite long, so when sitting down I could not reach to brace the door with my foot. I looked around and saw there was a long-handled brush leaning in the corner. I could sit with the brush held out in front with its head up against the door. That would do the trick. As the window opening had no glass in it, someone had kindly hung a bit of net curtain over the opening to give a sense of privacy.

It was quite a breezy morning and the curtain was horizontal, so not only was I having to hold the brush with one hand, I was also trying to hold down the flying net.

Now that was fine until I remember the cistern perched above my head. I could hear it filling. The rush of water was slowing and soon I would have to stand up and pull the chain yet again, which I could only just reach, as it was about two feet above my head when standing. I had to time it just right so that I wouldn't be drenched by the waterfall which would follow, or if I left it too late.

The family must have had a stopwatch or some sixth sense to tell them what was about to happen, as I could not keep hold of the curtain, the brush and at the same time pull the chain. I stood, brush under one arm, trousers at half mast with one arm raised and thrashing around in the air trying to catch hold of the chain, without looking up, in case I got an eye full of icy water, at that moment mother chose to pass to hang out the washing in the garden, or one of the girls had to go to the barn to get hen food. The other girls passed by on their way to catch to school bus, the farmer went to get something from the car, the postman or a rep from an animal feed supplier. They all seemed to pass my little room at some crucial moment.

They all looked in and said; "Good morning," in a light and cheerful voice; I found it most difficult to reply in the same vein.

The very last straw was when the farmer's wife, forgetting I was there, came and opened the door, which I then discovered opened outwards as well as inwards. What a sight - me holding the curtain and pointing the brush at her at the moment the cistern decided it would empty its contents.

For the rest of my stay I never bothered with any special precautions. I did what everyone else did. Whistled or sang, interrupted only by the occasional sound of a flushing loo!

One farm, in the depths of Wales, had what was descriptively known as a 'thunder box'. This was an outside toilet, where, on entering you were faced with a raised platform approximately eighteen inches high and eighteen inches wide, with a round hole cut usually in the middle to accommodate you in the sitting position. Below you would be a space with ashes or nettles or even a great drop it if was built on a hill. Sometimes if the building was large enough, there would be two holes, one a smaller one than the other to prevent children from falling into oblivion. Anyway, this particular one had two holes the same adult size, which I found to be most unusual.

So I said to the farmer; "At least if you are in a hurry you don't need to wait forever for someone to vacate, that's provided there is no conflict of personalities."

"That is so," he said. "But I find it's about the only time the wife and I can have a conversation in peace."

Enough said!

Driving back through Burton-upon-Trent found me in need of a loo. Being about 6pm, the traffic was very slow moving and, the slower it became, the worse my condition. My foot started to giggle up and down on the accelerator as I tried to drive cross-legged. Even the wishy washer container situated in the cab was full from a previous desperate situation (not to be recommended as operation of the washers causes multi-coloured streaks across the windscreen just before the workings seize up.

I'd thought about investing in an incontinence bag for just such an occasion but, like everything else, never quite got round to it.

Dear, oh, dear. I'm just about to do a very childish thing. But, hang on. The traffic seems to be moving a little quicker now. I am able to escape the confines of the town where I had not seen a public loo anywhere. At last, out into the country where I spot a lay-by with nearby trees. Oh, thank you.

There was one car in the lay-by with a man standing next to it. No matter. A very quick "good evening" and I'm hop skip and jumping into the foliage where I literally tear down my zip. Such relief. Let's be fair, there is nothing to compare.

So here I am in mid flow when I heard a voice shout out; "Are you coming, Mary?"

Where on earth was Mary? Not that it mattered. When you've got to go, you've got to go.

Isn't it strange how there's a toilet every five minutes after you've been?

TO THE DOGS

I met the farmer in the yard, after introducing myself I enquired; "Mr Shufflebottom?"

He replied; "Aye, sometimes."

He was not joking! This was a farm and a half, the farmer and his wife were the salt of the earth, working together as a team in pursuing their farming way of life. It all happened outside. They certainly were not into things domestic.

On first entering the house I could see it was the maids week off, for the past twelve years by the look of it. Sitting down, for example, proved difficult as the chairs were already occupied by heaps of *Farming News*, which tapered nicely from front to the back, converting the chairs conveniently into loungers. It was necessary to dig both heels in to stay put. I've heard of wiping your feet to go in, in this case you needed to wipe them to come out. This was the start of my stay with the couple. Being shown to the bedroom, where most would have used a hot water bottle to air the bed, no such luck here - this farm used the dog! As you can imagine I wasn't itching to go to bed that night.

When I did get to bed, sleep didn't come straight away, as there was a huge water tank in the room which appeared to fill only at night with a great spluttering, gurgling and rumbling. Due to the poor water supply and this tank also filled the animals water troughs, it wasn't until the beasts finished drinking there would be enough water pressure to fill the tank in my 'bedroom'. To try and abate the noise that I'm sure would have continued all night, I stood on the headboard in bare feet, like a bird, my hand in a cold wet tank holding the ball valve down, encouraging it to fill quickly, giving me a chance to get a bit of peace and sleep.

Morning eventually came and I rolled out of the 'pit' stark naked, half asleep and sat on the side of the bed facing the window with no curtains. Giving this fact no thought at all, until a voice shouted "Good Morning."

It was the farmer's wife walking past the window! Panic-struck, I slid onto the floor to finish dressing. Have you ever tried getting dressed lying on the floor?

Working and living on farms for the duration of a job could sometimes create difficulties for the farmer, particularly from the accommodation aspect. If the farmhouse is small, as can be with some of the smaller hill farms, or the farmer has a big family, then accommodation is a problem. You can almost hear them saying "where is he going to sleep?" But no matter what, farmers have always managed to put me up somehow.

On one particular occasion I was working on Mr Bell's farm. My accommodation arrangements were simple. I slept in the farmhouse and ate at the son's house next door. There was a drive maybe a hundred yards long between the two houses. The farm dog was resident in his kennel, which was at the farm end of the drive. He was very protective of his territory, on a long rope, and very alert. He never failed to surprise me. Every time I passed this stronghold, he would rush out of the kennel barking, often causing me to dive into the nearby hedge for protection, and at the same time thinking I must remember to proceed with caution next time. A battle of stealth, speed and wits developed during my stay, survival depended on my stealth and wits, and he had the speed!

My stay on the farm was drawing to an end, the milking equipment was operational and the first night's milking went without a hitch. The demonstrations of how to do it were over, farmer Bell had introduced his milking stock to their new lifestyle and all was well. As we stood back to take a final look at the gleaming installation, the warm feeling of success came over both of us, particularly Mr

Bell. He announced that there was just cause for celebration. After the evening meal he opened a bottle of Glen Mist, at least that's what it seemed like after a few good snifters.

Walking back to my sleeping accommodation much later, I remembered the dog. The Dutch courage must have been running well, because I headed straight for the dog kennel, and with authority!

I stuck my head into the kennel opening and shouted; "If you come out tonight, I'll have you."

With that I tottered off leaving the poor dog, no doubt, wondering what it was all about, cowering in the corner. The next morning found me feeling a little fragile and diving for cover yet again. I think the dog must have decided I wouldn't remember last night. How right he was!

As you may know, farmers usually have Border Collies for both sheep and cow dogs, these are advertised from time to time. So, when the need for new blood or a new dog is required, off the farmer goes to have a look. In this incident the dog was advertised as a working dog, so apart from settling down with its new owner it would not be long before it was earning its keep. A date was set and away the farmer went to check this animal out, with the prospects of returning home with it.

Much later he returned with no dog, I said; "wasn't the dog up to it then?"

He replied; "I'm not really sure."

"How do you mean?"

"Well, we had a talk, I looked the dog over and apart from being a tad nervous, it appeared to be in good order."

We more or less agreed on a price. I then asked if he would give me a demonstration of its ability. Off we went, into a field with a few sheep in it, these were in a group toward the top end. He stood there with his dog beside him and gave the command "away-by", the dog took off following the side of the hedge like a good-un, straight past, skirting the   flock as he should. I was thinking he's certainly not going to spook them. He didn't and we never saw hair or hide of him again." I said to yer man that was certainly some outrun, but I don't think I'll bother thank you." We walked back to the farm, never saying a word. He just went into the house slammed the door, no by your leave, or anything!

It is said a good working farm dog is worth its weight in gold. Sometimes I had my doubts. One farm I was working on had a Jack Russell rather than a collie. The farmer used to take this with him to round the cows up to bring them home for milking. He would set off with this little fellow trotting along beside him, no problem. I remember the first time I saw them take off and thinking that's a small dog to go rounding up cows with. I need not have worried. Not a long time after they had left, there was such a commotion with the cows coming up the track at a fair lick and farmer shouting and screaming. I was thinking he's certainly giving those cows what for, all came to light as soon as the herd came in to view, he was not admonishing the cows, it was the little dog! When bringing the cows in some dogs go behind the cows and just nip their ankles to help them on their way, especially if one or two were lagging behind. Not this little dog, he kept sneaking up behind the farmer and nipping his ankles. I wonder if this is how Morris dancing started out, it was one of the best renditions I had come across. He only needed the bells, he already had a stick.

I said to him; "Why do you take the dog, wouldn't it be less painful just on your own?"

"Yes, but I would spend more time checking other stock and general farming, this way I'm kept on my toes, literally, it gets the job done quicker."

It takes all sorts!

It was one howling winter's night, with everything outside clattering and banging, the kind of night you are glad to be indoors. Working farm dogs however, are usually kept in outbuildings or kennels that are normally fairly substantial. It needed to be on this particular night. I'm sure the dog didn't think so when the wind picked it up and dumped it on top of the nearby hedge, with him standing on his back tippytoes looking up at it. The chain being just long enough to save him from choking. A very happy dog to see its owner in the morning. This kennel was good and proper bolted down after that episode.

ME AND MINE

Accidents, illness, dental problems, even haircuts can all become exaggerated when you are away from home. In fact I don't believe cloning is anything new, especially when you saw the results of the mobile hairdresser –"next". In fact not to miss out, I volunteered to join the queue, one side was shorn when the telephone rang, the farmer said; "It's your wife for you, Ron."

Strange, it wasn't very often my wife checked up on me.

"Hello love, everything alright?"

"Well, I don't want you to panic or anything, but the house is on fire ("don't panic?")."

"Is everyone okay?"

"Yes."

"Oh, that's something, I'll be right home."

I turned to the hairdresser. "Excuse me would you mind finishing my hair cut please, I'm in a bit of a hurry."

After explaining to my hosts, that I would be back as soon as possible, away I went. You know when there is about one hundred miles between you and your home, by the time you get there it's more or less been sorted. It's one of these times you feel you should get a normal job. NAW!

On completing one installation on a Saturday morning, I would call at the hairdressers on the way home. It was an ideal time, no customers waiting, straight into the chair for a quick back and sides.

I was sat there nattering away when the barber says, "Did you used to work for the local milking machine company?"

(What's he on about, the van's stood outside!)

"Not any more mate, the buildings on fire and it's so bad, that they have had to abandon the local football match because of the danger of the smoke!"

With the amount of hair I have now, it isn't quite the same problem; it's a case of paying more for less!

Fortunately I wasn't often ill while away from home, I think it must have been a combination of plenty of good wholesome food and working outside with a roof on, or so it seemed. However, I think most of us succumbed to the Asian type 'flu at one time or another. For me it happened in North Yorkshire while staying with two of the nicest people you could ever inflict yourself on – 6 pm everything fine, 9pm I'm saying, "you will have to excuse me I don't feel too well."

That's the last time I moved for four days. This couple were elderly, which is why they were getting things made easier - or so they thought. There I am feeling very sorry for myself as men do, and these people with more than enough to do without chasing round after me like mother hens, making me feel ten times worse. After a few days of TLC, I start getting a little better, it's past bedtime and I have the urge to go to the toilet, so I wrap up and stagger downstairs to the little house, which is around the corner outside. There was no lighting in this convenience, so without a torch, it was more or less a 'hands on' experience. Eventually, I staggered back to my bedroom.

I'd not been in bed long when noises were heard outside the door, eventually the door opened slowly and a head popped round. "Oh, thank goodness you are back, are you alright? We were worried sick about you. We have been looking all over the place. We heard your door open and waited a while, then thought we had better go and see if we could find you, never thinking of looking in the toilet. We thought you had wondered off in a delirium."

That made me feel even worse (bless 'em). I recovered enough to complete the job, the time spent on the farm being rather longer than I, my wife, or the company anticipated.

When working in a very cramped area, such as a pump house, with large pipe grips manoeuvring into a suitable position can be a problem. Picture me on a platform approximately two feet off the ground, hands above my head hanging onto a pair of pipe grips, one foot on the shelf, the other one on the wall, pulling for all I'm worth trying to undo a fitting. Without warning the pipe broke, I took off backward at about a hundred knots (well, very fast), hitting the base of my spine on the door latch. It did more than bring tears to my eyes. I very gently made my way out of this little building on my hands and knees, to be met by the farmer's wife and daughter, who had been gardening at the time and had heard the bang with me saying things like "oh dear, oh dear" and "flipping heck". On seeing my appearance and obvious discomfort, not knowing where my very localised pain was, offered to take a look to see what they could do for me. This I am afraid I had to decline. Suffice to say it was difficult to concentrate on my work for a little while.

Now I'm not saying some of the spiders were big, probably because the ones in the cow shed eaves had not been disturbed for some time and had a chance of putting on a spot of weight. In some cases you could hear the dam things running. In one such situation on top of a fifteen-foot ladder, as well as keeping an eye on our hairy friends, my task was to make a hole through the wall. Running along this wall was a metal water pipe, the hole I was making needed to be just above this, so I rested my chisel on the pipe and hit it with my lump hammer (after many years of using a hammer and chisel you become very adept and really give the chisel some welly). This time was no different; the only thing was the brick I was knocking out was loose, allowing the chisel to shoot through the wall. My thumb hit the water pipe and my hammer hit my thumb, OW, OW, OW. This time I really descended the ladder very carefully.

I reached the bottom thinking, "I'm not going to look at my thumb." Being a born coward, I can stand any amount of comfort (but pain).

Sitting at the bottom of the ladder, my thumb in my mouth, then under my armpit and between my crutch, until finally building up enough courage to have a look, not a pretty sight. That certainly put an end to my installing for a while. My immediate problem was getting myself home, after a local doctor telling me my options were to have it off, or strapped up, with it being so badly damaged. I plumped for the latter, although after driving seventy miles home with my hand out of the window trying to cool it down, was it the best decision? I spent the following week with my thumb in iced water, again feeling very sorry for myself.

While working with a colleague on a difficult installation in Cockermouth, we would take it in turns to knock holes through the stone walls that are typical of that part of the country. In fact, when requiring a hole somewhere in the region of say, nine inch square, you often finish with an aperture big enough to fit a window instead. We had arrived in the evening as normal, ready to start work bright and early the following morning, or so I thought. My partner climbed out of bed and promptly collapsed in a heap on the floor, the dreaded 'flu strikes again.

He stayed in bed just long enough for me to knock all the holes out, these needing to be done on the onset of the installation in order to see how everything came together. No sooner had my partner emerged from his sick bed when I was struck down by the deadly lurgy. The only thing being my partner had a much easier time completing the job than I had starting it. Got it wrong again Dad.

ON THE ROAD

Finding farms was not usually a problem with them often situated in the wide open spaces. The ones near towns and villages could create more of a challenge. Normally a map would be used, if it was in or around a built up area it was often the case of using your tongue to find the destination.

This leads me to some of my encounters, for instance "Do you know where Mr Brown's farm is please?"

"Yes."

"Er, would you mind telling me?"

"No."

"Is that no you wouldn't mind? Or no you won't?"

Yes, he did tell me!!

"Could you tell me where Mr Atkinson's farm is please?"

"Well, you go up here right, then you turn right, right then you turn left right, then you turn left again right."

"Just a minute, I think you had better jump in and show me right."

Or, I was on a farm asking the directions to another farm and the farmer said; "Oh if I were you, wouldn't set off from here."

Excuse me?

It was quite a challenge finding my way around Northern Ireland. It was nearly always a matter of asking directions, partly because either there were not any road signs at all or if there were, they often faced in the opposite direction to where you wished to be. I believe this was to confuse the Army, or any one such as me from finding our way around. Also, when asking someone directions they would talk in townlands, this was the early way of denoting a district, and didn't bear any resemblance to the map I was carrying. They always asked which way did you come, I was wanting to know where I was going, not where I had been. After saying all that when asking an Irish farmer the way to another farm, no one anywhere could give more precise instructions, although on one occasion I was told to turn right where they had chopped the trees down.

You don't have to go abroad to be confused. I had travelled up to what is now Cumbria from the depot in Chester looking for a farm, stopping in the village of Bootle I asked a local if he knew where Mr Southward at Hall Waberthwaite lived.

"Niver here'd of him."

And me thinking I passed Bootle just outside Liverpool, one hundred and odd miles south from here.

Should I bite my knuckles or persevere?

"Mr Southward? Hall Waberthwaite?"

"Na."

"Just a minute I'll show you the address."

He read the address and his face lit up. "Tha means Joe Sutherd, from Waberthat."

Thank goodness for that!

Or, in Wales there I was struggling with an address and my director saying can you spell it, spell it? I can't even say it!!

Stopping at a bus stop once, I asked; "Does anyone know the way to Mr Easoms?"

In unison "We have no idea, sorry."

I said; "Well if you go up here and take the first turn right, then carry on for about half a mile then take a left, it's the first farm on the left."

They all thanked me!!

Then there was the travelling up some of the farm drives. This particular one seemed to go on for ever and I finally arrived into the yard to be greeted by the farmer and his son.

After introductions I said; "That is some drive you have there."

"Well you know," said he. "Me and lad here were only discussing that the other day, and we come to conclusion that if it wasn't that long, it wouldn't quite reach."

Ask a silly question.

Another time, in Eire, my Irish colleague and I were going up what can only be described as a cart track. It was atrocious as well as being very long. We avoided any pools of water as much as possible in case we disappeared without trace. Even so, the car bottomed out a few times. Having nowhere to turn we carried on to the bitter end, slowly and finally arriving at our destination, fortunately there was someone home, although I'm sure even they would not go out unless it was absolutely necessary.

My colleague's greeting went something like this "Excuse me Patrick, but do you use the AI (artificial insemination)?"

"I do, why do you ask?"

"Well I'm thinking you must get all heifer calves."

"What makes you say a thing like that?"

"It must shake the balls out of the bulls coming up the drive like that."

I believe the second word was "OFF".

On another first trip to a farm, this time with an agricultural agent, because the farmer was experiencing quite a lot of problems with a piece of equipment. The agent had called a few times, but the fault still persisted. The farmer was starting to get somewhat annoyed about this. I'm making conversation while travelling.

I happened to say; "what is the farmer like?"

Answer–"Put it this way, if he says it's dark, it's bloody dark."

Sorry I asked!

One of the fitters, whilst driving along suddenly realised he had to quickly attend to a call of nature. He happened to be driving rather fast through a built up area, when out jumped a policeman, who stopped him. "What's your hurry then?"

"I'm sorry officer, I'm looking for a toilet."

(Well he didn't exactly say toilet, it was something ending with house).

The policeman in turn said; "Get your driving licence out, you've just found one."

JACK AND MARY

One or two of the stories I did hear would be in the evening whilst we were sat relaxing after supper. This is one such tale.

Jack and Mary had gone to bed, when Mary said, "Did you bank the fire up Jack?"

"Er, no."

If this little job wasn't done it interrupted the general smooth running of the household, with a constant supply of hot water needed indoors and out. Or the porridge that was set on top the night before would not be ready in time, plus the kitchen and adjacent rooms would be cold next morning.

"Pop down and see to it Jack."

"No, you go," and so on. Anyway, Jack lost.

Now like many men, Jack kept his pajamas folded up on the bottom of the bed in case of fire; these stayed there while he proceeded down the stairs to carry out this little chore. In order to build this fire up, it was necessary to open the front door clip, a short handle on to the inner workings, and riddle the fire. This meant pulling and pushing the handle quite vigorously to remove the old cinders etc. This also necessitated bending over.

What Jack omitted to see was a kitten sat at the back of the kitchen. Well you can imagine it's little eyes when it saw all this activity and movement with bits and pieces swinging from side to side. It was all too much for this pussy, which shot across the room, leapt up and sank its claws, one in each globe. I think this action could have taken Jack by surprise. He in turn leapt into the air, quickly realising this wasn't the best course of action, the only way was to lower himself into a crouching position to take the weight off, while screaming for Mary to come and remove this 'cooking fat'. I must admit Jack had a strange expression on his face while this story enfolded.

I know it's rude to laugh at other people's misfortunes, but by this time I was rolling about on the floor. I have since wondered if Jack's pajamas were still folded up at the bottom of the bed.

AND SO TO BED

As mentioned in my early days, one or two of the farms were not on mains electricity, relying instead on a generator driven by a diesel or petrol engine for their needs. This was one such farm, the farmer was relating how he had moved on from using things like paraffin storm lamps and cooking on the stove etc, to this much more user friendly means of heat and light. One slight drawback –maintaining the engine - starting it up in the mornings and turning it off at night. When it was first installed he was a bit younger and a bit fitter. He had worked out that by turning the petrol supply off to the machine there was sufficient fuel left in the float chamber to keep the lights working for a little while before expiring. So, at bedtime he could go upstairs, undress, and don his pajamas then go back down to the engine house situated outside in a small outbuilding. By carefully making sure all was clear, he could turn the fuel supply off and be back upstairs and into bed before the light went out. This little exercise kept him fit.

That is until on one fateful night he missed seeing the cat on the stairs, because taking off from a standing start and slamming the doors behind him didn't leave a lot of time to check every detail, if he was going to make it to his bed in time, head over apex and crawled the rest of the way upstairs. He thought, there has to be an easier way than this, so he rigged up a series of pulleys and a string from the engine top tap and around the house right through into the bedroom, just lay in bed and pull the string –bliss. That was until on one of the worst nights you could ever come across, he climbed into bed pulled the string and it broke, tut tut.

Calling back at a later date, a mains supply had been installed, so no further ideas had to be put into practice.

Most people simply go to their bed same time, same place, each night, other than at times of special events and holidays. Imagine having a different area, family and mainly bedroom on every job.

Often this bedroom was borrowed from one of the younger children, who in turn would double up with a brother or sister. This arrangement usually worked well, it came unstuck when the child went to the loo at what could be 4am. The first I would know about this was a little hand in my face, followed very, very quickly by a high pitched scream.

You can appreciate my reaction, which was immediate - bolt upright in bed, eyes staring, matching scream for scream.

This was just the start of it. If there was two of us and you were not familiar with each other's sleeping habits, me hoping there would be separate bedrooms, which was not always the case, you could not even rely on separate beds. Oh dear, I had always looked upon myself as a man's man. The thought of sleeping with another fella had its reservations, to say the least, although its surprising how often this happened. One of my first experiences was a double bed and a trainee fitter, who was not only single but an only child.

I think I gained the upper hand, especially whilst asleep, I turned over and put my arm over him. I learned much later, he instantly awoke and laid petrified hoping this arm would either let go of him, or at least stay put.

One of my colleagues did say if you were in the situation of having to sleep with a fellow engineer, give him a kiss before turning in, it made sure you had a good night's sleep.

I was fast asleep one night, and was rudely awakened by what can only be described as the sound of a one-inch wide zip being pulled through an echo chamber. This is the explanation by my not too sleepy partner, was the curtains been drawn, he said he didn't want to wake me by switching the light on.

Your first night in a different house and bedroom was checking and remembering where the light switch is, especially when waking up in the middle of the night it is most embarrassing bumping into walls and furniture, or wondering down a hallway trying to remember which was the bathroom or on the way back looking for your bedroom - oops, excuse me, pardon me, I am sorry.

It was in one of these situations I found what could be termed as an untidy habit, namely putting clothes away neatly. As my want, I would take my clothes off, fold them up and throw them in a corner. This particular night was no different, after depositing my clothes on the floor, I set off across what was a very long narrow room, to switch off the lights. This done, I would then try to make it into bed before the light actually died completely. This particular bedroom had a highly polished floor. Between the light switch and the bed were my neatly crumpled clothes. As my stretched out foot made contact with soft material, my speed increased ten fold, my position altered from upright to horizontal instantly and I duly shot under the bed I was expecting to sleep on. The light switch came back on again along with a row of anxious faces, with a wry comment of; "I've heard of looking under the bed, etc."

I became quite tidy after this event.

After working all weekend away from home I was awakened at 6 am Monday with a very loud knocking on the bedroom door and an equally loud voice saying; "Get up you lazy so and so, day after tomorrow's Wednesday, that's half at week gone, and the's now't done yet."

While staying at a guest house in the Midlands, the landlady advised me to lock my bedroom door because Cynthia walks in her sleep. I went upstairs to take the door off its hinges! Well, I left it open a little bit. Sure enough, about two o'clock in the morning, the door creaked open and in walked Cynthia - WOW - the biggest flipping Alsation I had ever clapped eyes on. Just goes to show, nothing's quite as it seems.

Talking about going to bed, I was in bed one night when all of a sudden there was an almighty crash. It was so loud I nearly did a very childish thing! Gingerly switching the light on to see if there was anything untoward in my immediate surroundings, not finding anything and my bedroom walls were still standing, I decided to go back to sleep. I must admit this took more than a little while.

On going downstairs the next morning, the farmer's wife appeared very reserved whilst cooking breakfast. On looking around the kitchen the reason became quite apparent. The kitchen was a room with a false ceiling, and above was their bedroom. Sticking through the kitchen ceiling were four bed legs!!

I thought it prudent not to mention this, but the mystery of the loud noise had been solved. Now these two were not the smallest people you will have ever come across, I would guesstimate about the combined weight of a bullock and a half. The night before they had been larking about chasing one another around, both landing on the bed together, believe me something had to give.

The farmer entered the kitchen for his breakfast, while on his way through he flicked one of the casters saying; "It's certainly not going to go any farther, is it lass?"

It would be around one o'clock in the morning, I was sound asleep, when a voice woke me. My work mate was supposed to be asleep in the other bed, but I found him stood at the window saying things like; "who are you?" and; "no, you certainly cannot come in, go away."

He then left the window and went downstairs, leaving me thinking; "what the hecks happening?"

Sometime later, my mate returned shaking his head.

I asked; "What's to do?"

He replied; "Well, I woke up to hear this noise at the window, I hopped out of bed, opened the windows and nearly knocked this chap off a ladder propped up against the windowsill. We both got an L of a shock, with him nearly being knocked off and me just able to stop myself falling out after him. Apparently he's the son and it's his bedroom we are sleeping in. He's doing a course at agricultural college, so when he has some time off he jumps in his car and heads for home. If he arrives home late, he doesn't like to disturb the family and knowing his bedroom window is always open a little bit, he uses this method to get in - did he get a surprise - well, tonight after a little persuading, he has decided to sleep downstairs. We will sort it in the morning so we might as well get some sleep, goodnight."

I was in bed just about to settle down, when outside the dog starts barking, not just one of those "woof, woof, woofs", then stops, but one of those "BARK, BARK, BARK" all the time kind. I was laying there thinking if it doesn't shut up in a minute I am going to have to do something, the head under the pillow hasn't worked, counting up to 100 hasn't worked. BARK BARK BARK - Right, that is it, nothing for it, out of bed and over to the window. The next thing I am hanging out of the opening at 45 degrees, clinging onto the window - why? - because its chosen this moment to come away from its hinges. There I was, my toes clutching into the carpet, trying to stop myself from making a very untidy exit from the hole in the frame, whilst at the same time attempting to haul the window back into its rightful place. After much huffing and puffing, I managed to achieve the status quo. During all this time the dog has never uttered a peep. So off I go back to bed, wrecked. Less than five minutes later BARK BARK BARK! I'm back out of bed, but this time it's going to be face-to-face, so off I go in my majesty and my pajamas. Outside I'm making far more noise than the dog ever did. Finding a six foot railing, I throw it at the kennel "Now shut up". Back upstairs and to bed, five minutes later - silence, bliss.

The following morning I mentioned to the farmer I had an occasion to go down and have a word with his dog. "That's why we moved the kennel, we were not able to sleep because of it, also while we are on the subject, I would be very careful how you open the bedroom window as well!"

Having no idea what type of family we were going to encounter, we just got on with it. In this case things were a little different to the usual run of the mill. That's if there was such a thing. To begin with there were two of us, I mentioned this only happened occasionally, ie in training

149

or a difficult installation. We notice nearly straight away that this was going to be somewhat out of the ordinary.

To begin with, there were no papers, no radio, no TV. Also, nothing was eaten unless it was produced on the farm. After saying that, I think everything was eaten, brains, tripe, pigs cheek, trotters, squiggles etc. For two fellows in the habit of travelling around being pretty used to many and varied situations, it still came as a bit of a shock to see the college-aged daughters come down in a morning, and change from their night attire into their uniforms, partly because it was much warmer in the kitchen and also they had been brought up to believe it was nothing to worry about.

Maybe not to them, but for us it was very disconcerting, we didn't know where to look for the best, and how do you explain fork marks in your cheeks.

The beds were something else, the farmer made sure you didn't oversleep, that is if you slept at all. I'm sure its where he kept his seed potatoes. My partner said "do you think if I fold my hanky up, it will improve this pillow?" It couldn't make it much worse. What starts out as being funny soon wears off after a night or two, in fact we took it in turns to go home in the evening with the excuse we were short of equipment to keep the job going.

The first night we were working away when this voice shouted; "I'm away to bed now, your supper's on the table."

This became an anticlimax every evening, no not the supper, this apparition wearing a nightgown at 8.30pm telling us he was going to bed, he only needed a cap and a candle to be Wee Willy Winky! We would anticipate his arrival and have trouble containing ourselves until he had retired, then breaking down like big kids into fits of laughter. As I said, it takes all sorts.

It could be difficult to keep an open mind about things supernatural because some of the farm houses I stayed in can be best described as being a little eerie. For instance, while staying in one old farm house the bedroom had a kind of cold feisty smell to it, and this was during the summer. I'd put it down to the fact it had not been used for quite a while, even if it was known as the 'blue room'.

I'd just started dozing off when I head a tapping noise, must be a tree branch on the window, go to sleep. This proved to be difficult, so off I went to have a look. No, nothing near enough to be hitting the window. What can it be? It wasn't a regular tap, tap, tap, it was sort of intermittent and carried on throughout the night. So I had what you might call a restless sleep. Next morning when leaving my bedroom, I noticed in the hall upstairs that there was a part of the wall jutting like a chimney breast, but much deeper and wider. I went back into the bedroom to confirm that there were no signs of a chimney or fireplace, there wasn't. Talking to the family over breakfast, I mentioned by observation. It appeared the house had been modernised and one of the things that had been taken out was a spiral staircase and it had been replaced with a more traditional one. However, when spiral stairs were in place a coffin shoot was part of the original house, and rather than trying to do anything with it they bricked it up.

I said; "I don't like being an alarmist, but going by the noises I heard last night, I think someone's trying to escape." I felt it should have been me.

Another strange experience occurred while staying in a hotel. I was the only guest and the landlord and his wife had gone down to Oxford on a visit. The daughter-in-law looked after things until their return. After the last of the locals had departed, she would clear things away, lock up and return to her home, which was further into the village. The first night I was in bed reading my usual horror story when the sounds of a party in full swing filtered up to the bedroom. Knowing the hotel was empty, it must be some late-night revellers next door. You can imagine my surprise when looking out the next morning to find a blacksmith's shop on one side, a road at the front and fields on the other two sides; time I looked for alternative accommodation!

FINALLY

You can't often sometimes tell what's least expected most.

In other words:

I could baffle myself by the exuberance of my own philosophy.